SIMPLY VEGAN
QUICK VEGETARIAN MEALS

By Debra Wasserman

NUTRITION SECTION
By Reed Mangels, PhD, RD

5th Edition 2012
(1st Edition March 1991)

The VR.g VEGETARIAN *Resource Group*

**The Vegetarian Resource Group
Baltimore, Maryland**

Reed Mangels completed her Ph.D. in Nutrition at the University of Maryland. She has worked as a dietitian in hospitals and in the community. She has also taught college-level nutrition courses. Dr. Mangels is the author of the USDA's Nutri-Topics Bibliography on Vegetarian Diets. In addition, she has authored several papers for the Academy of Nutrition and Dietetics. Debra Wasserman earned an M.A. in International Relations from Georgetown University. She is co-director of The Vegetarian Resource Group, founding editor of Vegetarian Journal, and author of several vegan books.

ACKNOWLEDGMENTS

Special thanks to David Herring and Charles Stahler for reviewing sections of this book. Your encouragement and valuable comments added much to the final contents of this book. A big thanks goes to Keryl Cryer and John Cunningham who lent technical assistance. Thank you also to Janet Steinberg for doing the beautiful drawings found throughout this book and to Linda Long for shooting the photograph used on the front cover of this edition. And finally, thanks to friends and many members of The Vegetarian Resource Group who contributed, tasted, and commented on the recipes found in this book. These dishes were tested at potluck dinners, conferences, family gatherings, and other events over a two-year period.

© Copyright 2012, Debra Wasserman
Published by The Vegetarian Resource Group
PO Box 1463, Baltimore, MD 21203.

Cover photo by Linda Long; Illustrations by Janet Steinberg

Library of Congress Cataloging-in-Publication Data

Wasserman, Debra.
  Simply vegan : quick vegetarian meals / by Debra
Wasserman ; nutrition section by Reed Mangels, PhD, RD.
-- 5th edition.
      pages cm
  Includes bibliographical references and index.
  ISBN: 978-0-931411-34-2
  1. Vegan cooking. 2. Quick and easy cooking. I. Mangels,
Reed. II. Vegetarian Resource Group. III. Title.
  TX837.W323 2012
  641.5'636--dc23
                                                    2012035901

Printed in the United States of America

10 9 8 7 6 5 4 3 2 1

FOREWORD

Simply Vegan is more than a cookbook. It is a guide to a non-violent, environmentally sound, humane lifestyle.

Long ago, I became vegan for ethical reasons. As a graduate student studying International Relations at Georgetown University, I often found myself having to justify my strong beliefs in pacifism. In course after course on foreign policy making, I felt that I was the only one in my graduate class who saw war as the last option for settling disputes. With the exception of one other classmate from Venezuela, I was the only student who truly believed in promoting non-violence.

One evening as I sat around the dinner table with several non-vegetarian classmates, one person asked me if I ate meat. I replied, "yes." To which he added, "Isn't killing animals for food a violent act?" My response was that animals are not people. However, after that evening's discussion I immediately became vegetarian. I quickly realized that killing animals for food was not only unnecessary and inconsistent with my own non-violent lifestyle, but that raising animals for food was destroying our environment and in many cases ruining our health, too.

As time went on, I found eating a vegan diet, using ecologically sound products that have not been tested on animals, and wearing clothes made from non-animal sources to be simple, as long as you know where to shop for these items. Years ago I saw the need to create a convenient guide to vegan living. *Simply Vegan* is that resource. Now in its fifth edition, I hope this book makes your life simpler.

— **Debra Wasserman**
Baltimore, Maryland

Please Note: The contents of *Simply Vegan* are not intended to provide medical advice. Medical advice should be obtained from a qualified health professional.

TABLE OF CONTENTS

TIME-SAVING COOKING SUGGESTIONS

One purpose of *Simply Vegan* is to make vegan living as simple as possible. Most people follow a fast-paced lifestyle. Their hectic schedules leave them with little time to prepare elaborate vegan meals. Keeping this in mind, we have included the following time-saving cooking tips, as well as information on using microwave ovens. Although Debra Wasserman, author of *Simply Vegan*, doesn't own a microwave, others, including Dr. Karen Lazarus, a busy doctor and mother, frequently use microwave ovens to prepare vegan meals.

HOW TO COOK VEGETABLES QUICKER

== Slit green beans and carrots lengthwise
== Shred cabbage and beets
== Chop asparagus, broccoli, and cauliflower into flowerets
== Cube squash and potatoes; boil them instead of baking them
== Slice celery, bok choy, etc., on a 45 degree angle

OTHER TIME-SAVING IDEAS

== Use basmati rice; it cooks quicker than brown rice
== Use canned chickpeas (garbanzo beans), kidney beans, and other beans when in a rush; you may want to rinse out the salt from canned beans before cooking
== When cooking brown rice or potatoes, make extras to be used for preparing another meal

MICROWAVE COOKING

Debra Wasserman, the author of this book, rarely uses a microwave. On the other hand, Karen Lazarus finds microwave ovens to be a big time-saver, something she highly values while practicing medicine. Since we recognize that many households own a microwave oven today, we decided to present a section on the considerations associated with using microwave ovens to prepare food. The following information was written by Karen Lazarus, M.D.

At first I resisted buying a microwave oven. Perhaps it was because I had heard so much about safety problems in early models, or perhaps it was because I had heard that foods did not taste or look the same when cooked in a microwave oven. I had also heard microwave ovens described as expensive potato bakers. But I learned that they were tremendous time-savers, and the demands of my family and professional commitments eventually led me to purchase some time-saving appliances, including a microwave oven. Within a short time I wondered why I had waited so long to obtain such a valuable piece of equipment.

Microwave ovens are quick, convenient, cool, and energy-efficient appliances, that cook foods with a minimum of destruction to nutrients. As an example of its speed, one can bake a potato in 6-10 minutes, depending on its size. The rapid cooking preserves heat sensitive nutrients, as it is prolonged exposure to high temperatures that results in destruction of vitamins. Microwave ovens are convenient because of their speed, and because you can reheat, or even cook some items in the same dishes you will use to eat the foods, thereby avoiding the need to clean extra pots. When defrosting frozen foods, if you have frozen them in microwavable containers, you can just place the food in the container in the microwave oven.

Microwave ovens stay cool, which is especially great during summer. Even immediately after using it, both the outside and inside walls of the oven are safe to touch. However, although the dishes in which you cook will remain cooler than if placed in a conventional oven, they may become hot, especially with longer cooking, because of contact with the hot food. Even if you are able to remove a dish from the oven with your bare hands, you must remember to remove lids by opening the side away from you first to allow steam to escape on the other side, or you could burn yourself with the steam. Microwave ovens are energy efficient, using much less energy than a conventional oven, whether electric or gas.

Microwave ovens cannot completely replace other cooking methods. There will be no saving of time if you use a microwave oven to cook food that requires prolonged cooking for rehydration, such as pasta, rice, or dried beans, and you would need to use a very large bowl to prevent boiling over, so it is not worth using a microwave for these foods. Foods do not brown and become crisp in microwave ovens as they do in conventional ones; but on a vegan diet there are not as many foods that are browned as on an omnivorous diet.

Of all the foods that I have cooked in a microwave oven, there are only two that I can think of that do not come out as well as they do when cooked in a conventional oven. One is the skin of a baked potato. If I were given a choice, I would prefer a potato baked in the conventional oven because of the texture of the skin. However, at home I eat more microwave-baked potatoes because when I decide I want one, I usually do not want to wait over an hour to bake it, and I usually forget to put potatoes in my oven when I bake bread. I have never learned how to bake bread in a microwave oven, but it can be done. The second food that I prefer to bake in my conventional oven is a dessert made with fruit and matzoh which comes out crisp in my gas oven, and soft in the microwave oven. It probably tastes the same regardless of the cooking method, but the texture is different.

Finally, microwave cooking is not as even as other methods. In order to rectify this, some ovens are built with a turntable that spins automatically when the oven cooks.

Reed Mangels, Ph.D., R.D. adds: Here are guidelines for microwave cooking from the USDA Food Safety and Inspection Service and the FDA Center for Food Safety and Applied Nutrition: Only use cookware that is specially manufactured for use in the microwave oven. Glass, ceramic containers, and all plastics should be labeled for microwave oven use. Plastic storage containers such as margarine tubs, take-out containers, whipped topping bowls, and other one-time use containers should not be used in microwave ovens. These containers can warp or melt, possibly causing harmful chemicals to migrate into the food. Microwave plastic wraps, wax paper, cooking bags, parchment paper, and white microwave-safe paper towels should be safe to use. Do not let plastic wrap touch foods during microwaving. Never use thin plastic storage bags, brown paper or plastic grocery bags, newspapers, or aluminum foil in the microwave oven. (for more information see http://www.foodsafety.gov/blog/cook_it_safe.html)

INTRODUCING FAT AS A
PERCENTAGE OF DAILY VALUE

Since we first published *Simply Vegan*, food labels have been re-designed on packages. Fat as a percentage of Daily Value (% DV) is a figure being used on food labels today. It compares the grams of fat in a food to a total maximum amount of grams of fat that you should be consuming during a day. (Note that this "maximum" amount is a compromise acceptable to the general population. You may want to aim lower.)

Fat as a percentage of Daily Value was conceived as a simple way to give the person who knows little or nothing about grams of fat an idea as to whether a food is high or low in fat. There are actually two values on the new food labels: One for a person who eats 2,000 calories and one for a person who consumes 2,500 calories per day. So, while keeping track of grams of fat is probably the best way to watch your fat intake, the fat as a percentage of Daily Value can be helpful in determining if a food is high or low in fat.

For this book's fifth edition, we have analyzed the recipes based on the 2,000 calorie figure/65 grams of fat per day. Take our recipe for the Cauliflower and Carrots dish on page 52 as an example. It has 2 grams of fat. Based on 2,000 calories/65 grams of fat per day, if fulfills 3% of the Daily Value for fat (2 divided by 65 = 3%). You may want to eat less fat than the Daily Value of 65 grams, particularly if you eat fewer calories.

SAMPLE MENUS

BREAKFASTS

I. Cindy's Light and Fluffy Pancakes (p. 23)
    Peach Compote (p. 24)
    Sautéed Potatoes (p. 25)
    Orange Juice

II. Tofu/Squash Scramble (p. 97)
    Corn Bread (p. 21)
    Baked Pears (p. 26)
    Grape Juice

III. Oatmeal Plus (p. 23)
     Sliced Bananas or Apples
     Grape Juice or Soy milk

LUNCHES ON THE GO

I. Hummus (p. 27) on Pita Bread with Sprouts, Tomato, and
       Carrots
    Pineapple Juice
    Ginger Cookies (p. 109) and Plums

II. Fava Bean Spread (p. 28) on Whole Wheat Bread with
       Lettuce and Sliced Mushrooms
    Apple Nut Salad (p. 41)
    Popcorn Treat (p. 34)
    Orange Juice

III. Tofu Spread (p. 100) on Whole Wheat Crackers
     Cherry Tomatoes
     Grape Juice
     Apple

LUNCHES

I. Pasta Fruit Salad (p. 43)
    Corn Chowder (p. 45) and Pita Chips (p. 36)
    Thick Shake (p. 18)

II. Tempeh/Rice Pocket Sandwich (p. 94)
    Green Salad and Tangerine Dressing (p. 39) and Apple Juice
    Festive Cashew Cookies (p. 110)

III. Peanut Butter and Fruit (p. 29) on Whole Wheat Bread
     Carrot and Celery Sticks with Plain Soy Yogurt Dip
     Tomato Juice
     Karen's Creamy Rice Pudding (p. 115)

DINNERS

I. Carrot Salad
    Barbara's Kale Cream Sauce over Pasta (p. 91)
    Breaded Okra (p. 64)
    Fruit Whiz (p. 17) and Melon

II. Easy Coleslaw (p. 40)
    Fava Bean Delight (p. 78) and Lemony Rice (p. 54)
    Water or Juice
    Pita Chips (p. 36)

III. Apple Nut Salad (p. 41)
     Hummus (p. 27) Sandwich on Whole Wheat Bread with
         Sliced Tomato and Cucumber
     Corn Chowder (p. 45) and Grapes

IV. Stuffed Tomato Halves (p. 42)
    Barbecued Tempeh and Peaches (p. 95) with Plain Rice or
        Pasta
    Chocolate Pudding (p. 114)

V. Apple Celery Salad (p. 41)
    Wayne's Tofu Chili (p. 107) and Steamed Squash (p. 55) with
        Rice
    Baked Papaya (p. 112)

MENU ANALYSIS

(Note: Menus are on the preceding two pages.)

	Calories	Protein (gm)	Carb (gm)	Fat (gm)	Fat (% Daily Value)	Vit A (mg)
RDA **Male, 19-50**		**56**				**900**
Menu						
Breakfast 1	838	17	166	16	25	55
Breakfast 2	708	18	113	24	37	12
Breakfast 3	600	22	113	10	15	13
Go Lunch 1	648	16	126	13	20	693
Go Lunch 2	665	22	114	18	28	33
Go Lunch 3	439	11	81	10	15	335
Lunch 1	777	19	160	12	18	888
Lunch 2	921	30	139	30	46	41
Lunch 3	622	23	102	18	28	1814
Dinner 1	801	22	152	15	23	2234
Dinner 2	741	25	133	15	23	580
Dinner 3	746	22	131	23	35	772
Dinner 4	747	29	127	18	28	253
Dinner 5	733	27	142	10	15	486

Menu	Vit C (mg)	Thiamin (mg)	Ribo (mg)	Niac (mg)	Calcium (mg)	Iron (mg)
RDA Male, 19-50	90	1.2	1.3	16	1,000	8
Breakfast 1	121	1	0.4	7.4	256	4.7
Breakfast 2	9	0.5	0.4	3	331	10
Breakfast 3	16	1.9	0.9	5.3	151	5.6
Go Lunch 1	66	0.7	0.5	5.2	295	5.6
Go Lunch 2	123	0.6	0.4	5.5	193	5.3
Go Lunch 3	27	0.4	0.4	2.6	190	6.4
Lunch 1	84	0.7	0.6	4.9	184	5.1
Lunch 2	8	2.3	0.7	10.8	198	9.1
Lunch 3	64	0.6	0.4	8.1	184	6.2
Dinner 1	104	1.9	0.9	8.1	246	6.7
Dinner 2	135	0.7	0.4	5.8	232	6.1
Dinner 3	63	0.6	0.4	5.1	315	6.6
Dinner 4	51	0.6	0.5	9.4	232	5.9
Dinner 5	224	0.9	0.4	7	292	10.1

TOP 15 RECIPES FOR CALCIUM

		mg Ca/serving	Page #
1.	Tofu Casserole	279	105
2.	Spicy Sautéed Tofu with Peas	261	104
3.	Bok Choy Stir-Fry	240	63
4.	Mini Pizzas	235	34
5.	Cindy's Light and Fluffy Pancakes	195	23
6.	Broccoli and Tofu Sauté	194	103
7.	Pasta with Spicy Tahini Sauce	193	90
8.	Scrambled Tofu and Bok Choy	190	96
9.	Hummus	178	27
10.	Wayne's Tofu Chili	164	107
11.	Corn Bread	161	21
12.	Tofu Italiano	159	106
13.	Tofu Stew	153	104
14.	Tofu/Squash Scramble	151	97
15.	Tofu Spread	142	100

TOP 16 RECIPES FOR VITAMIN C

		mg Vitamin C/svg	Page #
1.	Tropical Fruit Smoothie	184	16
2.	Baked Papaya	118	112
3.	Blended Delight	112	18
4.	Wayne's Tofu Chili	90	107
5.	Cold Tomato Soup	86	48
6.	Red Hot Zucchini	77	56
7.	Fruit Whiz	75	17
8.	Sweet Orange Rice	73	53
9.	Broccoli Chow Mein	71	78
10.	Thick Shake	68	18
11.	Party Punch	67	19
12.	Mini Pizzas	67	34
13.	Fruit Fizz	55	19
14.	Broccoli and Tofu Sauté	53	103
15.	Bok Choy and Carrots	53	63
16.	Bok Choy and Apple	53	64

TOP 15 RECIPES FOR IRON

		mg Iron/svg	Page #
1.	Spicy Sautéed Tofu with Peas	14	104
2.	Tofu Casserole	9	105
3.	Tofu Italiano	9	106
4.	Tofu Stew	8	104
5.	Wayne's Tofu Chili	8	107
6.	Broccoli and Tofu Sauté	7	103
7.	Spicy Tofu Sauté	7	101
8.	Scrambled Tofu and Bok Choy	7	96
9.	Tofu/Squash Scramble	7	97
10.	Tofu Squash Burgers	7	102
11.	Creamed Broccoli and Pasta	6	86
12.	Tofu Mushroom Sauce	6	101
13.	Tofu Dip	6	99
14.	Creamy Lentil Soup	6	49
15.	Tofu "Coddies"	6	102

RECIPES

Recipe analysis was done with the Nutripak Professional Plus System (Nutrient Data Resources, Cleveland, Ohio) with additional information from manufacturers and food composition tables (1,2).

Optional ingredients were not included in calculations. For a range of servings such as 2-3, the lower number of servings was selected.

1. Lanza E and Butrum RR: A critical review of food fiber analysis and data. *Journal of the American Dietetic Association*, 86:732-743, 1986.

2. Hurlbert I and Liebman B: Rough it up. *Nutrition Action*, 17:8-9, 1990.

BEVERAGES

TROPICAL FRUIT SMOOTHIE

(Serves 2)

2 kiwi fruit, peeled
3 oranges, peeled and seeded
1 banana, peeled
6 ice cubes

Place all the ingredients in a blender and blend until smooth. Serve immediately.

Variations: Substitute different fruits such as pineapple, strawberries, or grapes.

TOTAL CALORIES PER SERVING: 192   TOTAL FAT AS % OF DAILY VALUE: 2%
PROTEIN: 3 gm   CARBOHYDRATES: 48 gm   FAT: 1 gm
CALCIUM: 102 mg   IRON: 0.7 mg   SODIUM: 5 mg   DIETARY FIBER: 6 gm

FRUIT WHIZ

(Serves 2)

1 Cup soy milk
1 teaspoon vanilla extract
2 large oranges, peeled and sectioned
1 large banana, peeled
5 ice cubes

Place all the ingredients in a blender and blend until smooth. Serve immediately.

Variation: Substitute 3 peeled tangerines for the oranges. Make sure to remove all seeds before blending.

TOTAL CALORIES PER SERVING: 192   TOTAL FAT AS % OF DAILY VALUE: 6%
PROTEIN: 7 gm   CARBOHYDRATES: 36 gm   FAT: 4 gm
CALCIUM: 98 mg   IRON: 1 mg   SODIUM: 66 mg   DIETARY FIBER: 4 gm

BLENDED DELIGHT

(Serves 4)

2 bananas, peeled
1 peach, peeled and pitted
6 strawberries
4 Cups orange juice

Place all the ingredients in a blender and blend until smooth. Chill and serve.

Variations: Substitute blueberries for strawberries and/or different fruit juices for orange juice.

TOTAL CALORIES PER SERVING: 178   TOTAL FAT AS % OF DAILY VALUE: <1%
PROTEIN: 3 gm   CARBOHYDRATES: 44 gm   FAT: <1 gm
CALCIUM: 29 mg   IRON: 1 mg   SODIUM: 3 mg   DIETARY FIBER: 3 gm

THICK SHAKE

(Serves 3)

1-1/2 Cups soy milk
1 teaspoon vanilla extract
1 papaya, peeled and chopped
1 banana, peeled
1 Cup raisins

Place all the ingredients in a blender and blend until smooth. Serve immediately.

Variation: Substitute 2 peaches for the papaya.

TOTAL CALORIES PER SERVING: 317   TOTAL FAT AS % OF DAILY VALUE: 6%
PROTEIN: 8 gm   CARBOHYDRATES: 69 gm   FAT: 4 gm
CALCIUM: 96 mg   IRON: 2 mg   SODIUM: 75 mg   DIETARY FIBER: 6 gm

PARTY PUNCH

(Serves 4)

1 pint cranberry juice
1 pint lemonade
Liter bottle of ginger ale or club soda
1 orange, sliced and seeds removed
Ice

Mix all the ingredients in a large punch bowl and serve.

Variations: Use different juices and/or replace orange slices with lemon slices.

TOTAL CALORIES PER SERVING: 222   TOTAL FAT AS % OF DAILY VALUE: <1%
PROTEIN: <1 gm   CARBOHYDRATES: 57 gm   FAT: <1 gm
CALCIUM: 28 mg   IRON: 1 mg   SODIUM: 23 mg   DIETARY FIBER: <1 gm

FRUIT FIZZ

(Serves 2)

5 ounces crushed pineapple
1 Cup orange juice
1 apple, peeled, diced, and cored
1 pear, peeled, diced, and cored
14 ounces club soda

Place all the ingredients in a blender and blend until smooth. Chill and serve.

TOTAL CALORIES PER SERVING: 163   TOTAL FAT AS % OF DAILY VALUE: <1%
PROTEIN: 1 gm   CARBOHYDRATES: 41 gm   FAT: <1 gm
CALCIUM: 33 mg   IRON: <1 mg   SODIUM: 48 mg   DIETARY FIBER: 4 gm

BREAKFASTS

APPLE RAISIN SPICE MUFFINS

(Makes 18)

1 Cup unbleached white flour
2 Cups whole wheat pastry flour
1 teaspoon baking powder
1/2 teaspoon baking soda
1 teaspoon cinnamon
1/4 teaspoon nutmeg
1/2 teaspoon allspice
1 Cup water
1/3 Cup maple syrup or molasses
2 apples, cored and chopped finely
1/2 Cup raisins

Preheat oven to 400 degrees. Mix all the ingredients together in a large bowl. Pour batter into lightly oiled muffin tins. Bake for 20 minutes at 400 degrees.

Cool muffins before removing from tins.

Variation: Add 1/2 cup chopped walnuts to batter before baking.

TOTAL CALORIES PER MUFFIN: 106   TOTAL FAT AS % OF DAILY VALUE: <1%
PROTEIN: 3 gm   CARBOHYDRATES: 24 gm   FAT: <1 gm
CALCIUM: 20 mg   IRON: <1 mg   SODIUM: 32 mg   DIETARY FIBER: 2 gm

BANANA MUFFINS

(Makes 18)

4-5 bananas (approximately 2 Cups)
1 Cup raisins (If hard, soften by soaking in apple juice.)
3 Cups rolled oats
1 Tablespoon cinnamon
1 Tablespoon baking powder
1/2 Cup almond or peanut butter

Preheat oven to 350 degrees. Mash bananas. Add the remaining ingredients and mix well. Pour batter into lightly oiled muffin tins. Bake 25 minutes at 350 degrees. Cool muffins before removing from tins.

Variation: Substitute 1/3 cup oil for nut butter.

TOTAL CALORIES PER MUFFIN: 154   TOTAL FAT AS % OF DAILY VALUE: 8%
PROTEIN: 4 gm   CARBOHYDRATES: 25 gm   FAT: 5 gm
CALCIUM: 61 mg   IRON: 1 mg   SODIUM: 3 mg   DIETARY FIBER: 3 gm

CORN BREAD

(Serves 6)

1 Cup cornmeal
1 Cup whole wheat flour
1 Tablespoon baking powder
1/4 Cup oil
1 Cup soy milk
1/3 Cup molasses or maple syrup

Preheat oven to 375 degrees. Mix ingredients together in a bowl. Pour batter into lightly oiled 8-inch round pan. Bake for 20 minutes.

Variation: Prepare same batter; however, pour batter into lightly oiled muffin tins and bake at the same temperature for the same amount of time. Children will especially enjoy these muffins.

TOTAL CALORIES PER SERVING: 299   TOTAL FAT AS % OF DAILY VALUE: 17%
PROTEIN: 6 gm   CARBOHYDRATES: 46 gm   FAT: 11 gm
CALCIUM: 161 mg   IRON: 3 mg   SODIUM: 29 mg   DIETARY FIBER: 2 gm

OATMEAL MEDLEY

(Serves 4)

2 Cups rolled oats
4 Cups water
1/2 Cup unsweetened shredded coconut
1/2 teaspoon cinnamon
1 Cup fresh or frozen blueberries

Mix ingredients (except for blueberries) together in a pot. Cook over medium heat for about 10 minutes until oats are done. Stir oats occasionally while cooking.

Add blueberries and heat for 3 more minutes. Serve hot.

Variation: Substitute strawberries or other chopped fruit for blueberries.

TOTAL CALORIES PER SERVING: 244   TOTAL FAT AS % OF DAILY VALUE: 14%
PROTEIN: 8 gm   CARBOHYDRATES: 34 gm   FAT: 9 gm
CALCIUM: 28 mg   IRON: 2 mg   SODIUM: 6 mg   DIETARY FIBER: 4 gm

OATMEAL PLUS

(Serves 2)

1/2 Cup rolled oats
1 Cup water
1/8 Cup nutritional yeast
1/4 Cup wheat germ
1 Cup soy milk

Place oats and water in large microwaveable bowl (at least 1 quart size). Microwave on high for 4 minutes and 10 seconds (or cook in pot on stove until thickened). Add nutritional yeast, wheat germ, and soy milk. Mix together.

Variation: Add raisins or other dried fruit.

TOTAL CALORIES PER SERVING: 211   TOTAL FAT AS % OF DAILY VALUE: 9%
PROTEIN: 14 gm   CARBOHYDRATES: 28 gm   FAT: 6 gm
CALCIUM: 76 mg   IRON: 4 mg   SODIUM: 76 mg   DIETARY FIBER: 3 gm

CINDY'S LIGHT AND FLUFFY PANCAKES

(Serves 4)

2 Cups whole wheat pastry flour
1/2 Cup cornmeal
2 Tablespoons Ener-G Egg Replacer or cornstarch
2 teaspoons baking powder
1/2 teaspoon baking soda
1/2 teaspoon cinnamon
2 Tablespoons oil
1 Cup each lowfat soy milk and water
1/8 Cup maple syrup
1/4 teaspoon apple cider vinegar

Mix dry ingredients together. Then add the remaining ingredients.

Make sure all the ingredients are mixed together well. Batter should be spongy — not runny or thick. Preheat lightly oiled frying pan over medium heat. Pour a ladle full of batter into pan and cook on both sides until golden brown. Makes 5 large pancakes.

(Note: Ener-G Egg Replacer can be purchased at some natural foods stores or through the mail. See page 208.)

TOTAL CALORIES PER SERVING: 385   TOTAL FAT AS % OF DAILY VALUE: 14%
PROTEIN: 11 gm   CARBOHYDRATES: 71 gm   FAT: 9 gm
CALCIUM: 195 mg   IRON: 3 mg   SODIUM: 146 mg   DIETARY FIBER: 5 gm

PEACH COMPOTE

(Serves 3)

3 peaches, pitted and chopped
1/3 Cup raisins
2 Tablespoons apple juice concentrate
2 Tablespoons water

Heat all the ingredients together over medium-high heat for 3 minutes. Lower heat and simmer for 20 minutes longer. Serve hot over pancakes or French toast.

TOTAL CALORIES PER SERVING: 111   TOTAL FAT AS % OF DAILY VALUE: <1%
PROTEIN: 1 gm   CARBOHYDRATES: 29 gm   FAT: <1 gm
CALCIUM: 16 mg   IRON: <1 mg   SODIUM: 3 mg   DIETARY FIBER: 3 gm

FRUIT FRENCH TOAST

(Serves 2)

1 banana, peeled
4 large strawberries, fresh or frozen
1/3 Cup apple juice
1/2 teaspoon cinnamon
4 slices whole wheat bread

Blend together first four ingredients. Soak bread in the fruit mixture. Cook on both sides on lightly oiled or non-stick griddle until just beginning to brown.

Variation: Use other fruits such as pineapple or blueberries.

TOTAL CALORIES PER SERVING: 191   TOTAL FAT AS % OF DAILY VALUE: 3%
PROTEIN: 6 gm   CARBOHYDRATES: 42 gm   FAT: 2 gm
CALCIUM: 55 mg   IRON: 2 mg   SODIUM: 243 mg   DIETARY FIBER: 5 gm

SAUTÉED POTATOES

(Serves 4)

6 potatoes, cleaned and thinly sliced
2 Tablespoons oil
1 onion, finely chopped
1/2 teaspoon garlic powder
1/4 teaspoon paprika
Pepper and salt to taste

Stir-fry ingredients together in a large frying pan for 20 to 25 minutes over medium-high heat until potatoes are tender. Stir often so potatoes do not stick to pan. Serve hot.

TOTAL CALORIES PER SERVING: 243   TOTAL FAT AS % OF DAILY VALUE: 11%
PROTEIN: 4 gm   CARBOHYDRATES: 42 gm   FAT: 7 gm
CALCIUM: 22 mg   IRON: <1 mg   SODIUM: 11 mg   DIETARY FIBER: 4 gm

FRIED BANANAS

(Serves 2)

3 very ripe bananas, peeled
1 Tablespoon oil
1/4 teaspoon cinnamon

Heat oil in a frying pan over medium heat. Slice bananas in half length-wise. Lay bananas in pan. Sprinkle with cinnamon. Fry on each side for 2 minutes. Serve hot.

TOTAL CALORIES PER SERVING: 218   TOTAL FAT AS % OF DAILY VALUE: 12%
PROTEIN: 2 gm   CARBOHYDRATES: 40 gm   FAT: 8 gm
CALCIUM: 10 mg   IRON: <1 mg   SODIUM: 2 mg   DIETARY FIBER: 2 gm

BAKED PEARS

(Serves 2)

2 large pears, cored and sliced
1 teaspoon cinnamon
1/4 Cup water

Preheat oven to 425 degrees. Lay pears in a baking pan. Sprinkle with cinnamon and water. Bake for 25 minutes at 425 degrees. Serve hot.

Variation: Add raisins before baking.

TOTAL CALORIES PER SERVING: 98   TOTAL FAT AS % OF DAILY VALUE: <1%
PROTEIN: <1 gm   CARBOHYDRATES: 25 gm   FAT: <1 gm
CALCIUM: 18 mg   IRON: <1 mg   SODIUM: 0 mg   DIETARY FIBER: 6 gm

SANDWICHES

CHICKPEA ITALIANA

(Makes 6 sandwiches)

19-ounce can chickpeas or garbanzo beans, drained
    and mashed
1/4 teaspoon oregano
1/8 teaspoon pepper
1/4 teaspoon onion powder
4 Tablespoons tomato sauce

Mix all the ingredients in a bowl. Serve on whole wheat bread with lettuce.

TOTAL CALORIES PER SERVING SPREAD: 98 TOTAL FAT AS % OF DAILY VALUE: 2%
PROTEIN: 4 gm   CARBOHYDRATES: 19 gm   FAT: 1 gm
CALCIUM: 27 mg   IRON: 1 mg   SODIUM: 301 mg   DIETARY FIBER: 3 gm

HUMMUS

(Makes 6 sandwiches)

1 large onion, chopped
2 cloves garlic, minced
1/4 Cup water
19-ounce can chickpeas or garbanzo beans, drained
1/2 Cup tahini (sesame butter)
1/4 Cup lemon juice or juice from 1 fresh lemon
1/4 teaspoon pepper
1/8 teaspoon cayenne pepper
1/3 Cup chopped parsley (optional)
3 Tablespoons water

Sauté onion and garlic in oil until onion is transparent. Pour into a blender or food processor. Add remaining ingredients. Blend until mixture is smooth, adding a little more water if necessary. Serve on whole wheat bread or in pita bread with chopped lettuce or sprouts and tomato, or as a dip with raw vegetables and crackers.

TOTAL CALORIES PER SERVING SPREAD: 182
TOTAL FAT AS % OF DAILY VALUE: 12%
PROTEIN: 7 gm   CARBOHYDRATES: 26 gm   FAT: 8 gm
CALCIUM: 178 mg   IRON: 2 mg   SODIUM: 280 mg   DIETARY FIBER: 5 gm

GARBANZO SPREAD

(Makes 6 sandwiches)

19-ounce can garbanzo beans (chickpeas), drained
1/2 Cup tomato sauce
1-2 teaspoons cumin
1-2 teaspoons garlic powder

Blend all the ingredients together in a blender or food processor. Serve on whole wheat bread with lettuce.

TOTAL CALORIES PER SERVING SPREAD: 102
TOTAL FAT AS % OF DAILY VALUE: 2%
PROTEIN: 4 gm   CARBOHYDRATES: 20 gm   FAT: 1 gm
CALCIUM: 28 mg   IRON: 1 mg   SODIUM: 363 mg   DIETARY FIBER: 1 gm

FAVA BEAN SPREAD

(Makes 6 sandwiches)

19-ounce can fava beans, drained
1/4 Cup tahini (sesame butter)
1 Tablespoon lemon juice
1 teaspoon garlic powder

1 Tablespoon olive oil
1/4 Cup water

Blend all the ingredients together in a blender or food processor until smooth. Serve on whole wheat bread with lettuce.

TOTAL CALORIES PER SERVING SPREAD: 120
TOTAL FAT AS % OF DAILY VALUE: 9%
PROTEIN: 6 gm   CARBOHYDRATES: 14 gm   FAT: 6 gm
CALCIUM: 95 mg   IRON: 2 mg   SODIUM: 406 mg   DIETARY FIBER: 4 gm

PEANUT BUTTER AND FRUIT

(Makes 1 sandwich)

1 Tablespoon peanut butter
1/2 fresh fruit (apple, pear, banana, etc.), thinly sliced
2 slices bread

Spread peanut butter on your favorite bread. Place slices of fresh fruit on the peanut butter. Enjoy!

Variation: Substitute dried fruit (apricots, figs, apples, pears, raisins, etc.) for the fresh fruit.

TOTAL CALORIES PER SANDWICH: 258   TOTAL FAT AS % OF DAILY VALUE: 17%
PROTEIN: 10 gm   CARBOHYDRATES: 36 gm   FAT: 11 gm
CALCIUM: 46 mg   IRON: 2 mg   SODIUM: 394 mg   DIETARY FIBER: 6 gm

HOT BEAN SPREAD

(Makes 2-3 sandwiches)

1 Cup homemade or canned vegetarian baked beans
1 Tablespoon horseradish or more if desired
1/2 small onion, minced

Mash the beans in a bowl. Add the horseradish and onion. Mix well. Spread on two slices of whole wheat bread. Serve with lettuce and tomato slices.

TOTAL CALORIES PER SERVING SPREAD: 112
TOTAL FAT AS % OF DAILY VALUE: 2%
PROTEIN: 6 gm   CARBOHYDRATES: 25 gm   FAT: 1 gm
CALCIUM: 51 mg   IRON: 1 mg   SODIUM: 423 mg   DIETARY FIBER: 9 gm

SWEET BEAN SPREAD

(Makes 2-3 sandwiches)

1 Cup homemade or canned vegetarian baked beans
2 Tablespoons sweet pickle relish

Mash the beans in a bowl. Add the relish and mix well. Spread on whole wheat bread and add a few lettuce leaves.

TOTAL CALORIES PER SERVING SPREAD: 120
TOTAL FAT AS % OF DAILY VALUE: 2%
PROTEIN: 5 gm   CARBOHYDRATES: 27 gm   FAT: 1 gm
CALCIUM: 43 mg   IRON: 1 mg   SODIUM: 518 mg   DIETARY FIBER: 9 gm

APPLE BEAN SPREAD

(Makes 8 sandwiches)

19-ounce can white kidney beans or other white beans
4 Delicious apples, peeled, cored, and chopped
1/4 teaspoon cinnamon

Drain the beans. Place all the ingredients in a food processor. Blend at high speed until creamy. If time, chill first and then serve on whole wheat bread or with lowfat crackers.

TOTAL CALORIES PER SERVING SPREAD: 89
TOTAL FAT AS % OF DAILY VALUE: <1%
PROTEIN: 4 gm   CARBOHYDRATES: 19 gm   FAT: <1 gm
CALCIUM: 33 mg   IRON: 1 mg   SODIUM: 219 mg   DIETARY FIBER: 3 gm

OAT NUT BURGERS

(Makes 6)

2/3 Cup each rolled oats and chopped walnuts
1 large onion, chopped
3 stalks celery, chopped
2 carrots, grated
1/4 Cup whole wheat pastry or unbleached white flour
1/4 Cup water

Mix the ingredients together and season to taste. Shape into 6 burgers and fry 10 minutes over medium-heat on each side until brown.

TOTAL CALORIES PER BURGER: 156   TOTAL FAT AS % OF DAILY VALUE: 14%
PROTEIN: 6 gm   CARBOHYDRATES: 16 gm   FAT: 9 gm
CALCIUM: 33 mg   IRON: 1 mg   SODIUM: 27 mg   DIETARY FIBER: 3 gm

GARBANZO BEAN BURGERS

(Makes 6)

2 Cups garbanzo beans (chickpeas), mashed
1 stalk celery and 1 carrot, finely chopped
1/4 small onion, minced
1/4 Cup whole wheat flour
Salt and pepper to taste
2 teaspoons oil

Mix the ingredients (except oil) in a bowl. Form 6 flat patties. Fry in oiled pan over medium-high heat until burgers are golden brown on each side.

TOTAL CALORIES PER BURGER: 133   TOTAL FAT AS % OF DAILY VALUE: 5%
PROTEIN: 5 gm   CARBOHYDRATES: 23 gm   FAT: 3 gm
CALCIUM: 34 mg   IRON: 1 mg   SODIUM: 250 mg   DIETARY FIBER: 2 gm

SNACKS

GARLIC BEAN DIP

(Serves 2)

1/3 pound green beans
2 cloves garlic, minced
1/2 teaspoon onion powder
1-1/2 Tablespoons tahini (sesame butter)
1 teaspoon soy sauce or tamari

Steam green beans for 10 minutes in about a cup of water until tender, yet firm. Rinse beans under cold water when done. Meanwhile, place remaining ingredients in a blender or food processor. Add cooked beans. Blend 2 minutes or until creamy. Serve with crackers.

TOTAL CALORIES PER SERVING: 69   TOTAL FAT AS % OF DAILY VALUE: 6%
PROTEIN: 3 gm   CARBOHYDRATES: 9 gm   FAT: 4 gm
CALCIUM: 121 mg   IRON: 1 mg   SODIUM: 203 mg   DIETARY FIBER: 3 gm

SPICY NACHO "CHEESE" DIP

(Serves 8)

1-1/2 Cups nutritional yeast
2/3 Cup whole wheat pastry or unbleached white flour
2-1/2 Cups water
3 Tablespoons vegan soy margarine
1 teaspoon garlic powder
1 Tablespoon mustard
1/3 Cup hot cherry peppers, diced

Mix yeast, flour, and water together in a pot. Cook over medium heat, stirring occasionally, until mixture boils. Add margarine. Allow to boil for one minute, then remove from heat.

Add garlic powder, mustard, and hot cherry peppers. Mix well.

Serve hot or chilled with crackers, chips, or raw vegetables.

TOTAL CALORIES PER SERVING: 146   TOTAL FAT AS % OF DAILY VALUE: 8%
PROTEIN: 11 gm   CARBOHYDRATES: 18 gm   FAT: 5 gm
CALCIUM: 62 mg   IRON: 5 mg   SODIUM: 90 mg   DIETARY FIBER: <1 gm

QUICK SALSA

(Serves 8)

29-ounce can tomato purée
2 ripe tomatoes, chopped
1 green pepper, chopped
4 scallions, chopped
1/4 teaspoon cayenne pepper
1 teaspoon garlic powder
Salt to taste (optional)

Mix all the ingredients together in a large bowl. Serve with chips.

Variation: Add more cayenne pepper to make salsa hotter!

TOTAL CALORIES PER SERVING: 44   TOTAL FAT AS % OF DAILY VALUE: <1%
PROTEIN: 2 gm   CARBOHYDRATES: 10 gm   FAT: <1 gm
CALCIUM: 25 mg   IRON: 1 mg   SODIUM: 670 mg   DIETARY FIBER: 2 gm

POPCORN TREAT

(As many servings as you would like)

Popcorn
Nutritional yeast, to taste

Pop popcorn in an air popper until done. Sprinkle with nutritional yeast.

TOTAL CALORIES PER 3 CUP SERVING: 138   TOTAL FAT AS % OF DAILY VALUE: 3%
PROTEIN: 5 gm   CARBOHYDRATES: 28 gm   FAT: 2 gm
CALCIUM: 4 mg   IRON: 1 mg   SODIUM: 0 mg   DIETARY FIBER: 3 gm

MINI PIZZAS

(Serves 2-3)

1 stalk broccoli, chopped
2 stalks celery, chopped finely
1 onion, minced
1/2 teaspoon oregano
1/2 teaspoon garlic powder
1/3 Cup water
15-ounce can no salt added tomato sauce
3 English muffins containing no animal products

Sauté broccoli, celery, onion, oregano, and garlic powder in water over medium-high heat for 5 minutes, until broccoli is tender, yet firm. Add tomato sauce and continue heating for 3 minutes longer. Remove from heat.

Split English muffins in half. Spoon sauce over muffins. Sprinkle with nutritional yeast if desired.

Bake at 400 degrees for 12 minutes. Serve pizza hot.

Variation: Substitute different vegetables in sauce such as mushrooms, green pepper, cauliflower, etc.

TOTAL CALORIES PER SERVING: 314   TOTAL FAT AS % OF DAILY VALUE: 3%
PROTEIN: 13 gm   CARBOHYDRATES: 65 gm   FAT: 2 gm
CALCIUM: 235 mg   IRON: 5 mg   SODIUM: 860 mg   DIETARY FIBER: 6 gm

COCONUT CHAPPATIS

(Serves 2)

1/2 Cup whole wheat pastry or unbleached white flour
1/3 Cup shredded coconut
1/2 teaspoon cinnamon
4 Tablespoons water

Mix ingredients together to form a firm dough. Divide into 4 equal parts. On floured board, roll each piece into a 1/4-inch thick circle.

Cook chappatis in an oiled pan over medium heat until light brown on each side. Serve warm.

TOTAL CALORIES PER SERVING: 181   TOTAL FAT AS % OF DAILY VALUE: 14%
PROTEIN: 5 gm   CARBOHYDRATES: 23 gm   FAT: 9 gm
CALCIUM: 19 mg   IRON: 2 mg   SODIUM: 4 mg   DIETARY FIBER: unknown

SPLIT PEA DIP

(Serves 6)

3-1/4 Cups water
1 Cup split peas
1 carrot, finely chopped
2 stalks celery, finely chopped
1 small onion, chopped
1 teaspoon celery seed
Salt and pepper to taste

Bring split peas and water to a rapid boil. Add remaining ingredients and boil for another 15 minutes. Remove from heat. Place mixture in food processor and blend until smooth. If time, chill before serving with raw vegetables.

TOTAL CALORIES PER SERVING: 98   TOTAL FAT AS % OF DAILY VALUE: <1%
PROTEIN: 6 gm   CARBOHYDRATES: 18 gm   FAT: <1 gm
CALCIUM: 19 mg   IRON: 1 mg   SODIUM: 26 mg   DIETARY FIBER: 3 gm

PITA CHIPS

(Serves 8)

3 pita breads
2 teaspoons oil
1 teaspoon paprika
1 teaspoon garlic powder
1 teaspoon oregano
1/2 teaspoon salt (optional)

Split pita breads in half. Cut each half into several 2-inch size triangles.

Place the cut bread on a lightly oiled cookie sheet. Sprinkle bread with half the oil, and half the paprika, garlic powder, oregano, and if you prefer, salt.

Place the bread under a broiler until it begins to brown. Turn the bread over and sprinkle with remaining oil and spices. Place the bread back under the broiler for 2 minutes longer. Remove the chips. Once the chips cool they will be crisp and delicious.

TOTAL CALORIES PER SERVING: 49   TOTAL FAT AS % OF DAILY VALUE: 2%
PROTEIN: 2 gm   CARBOHYDRATES: 8 gm   FAT: 1 gm
CALCIUM: 12 mg   IRON: <1 mg   SODIUM: 81 mg   DIETARY FIBER: <1 gm

CHEESY PITA TOAST

(Serves 2)

2 pita breads
2 Tablespoons nutritional yeast
1 Tablespoon vegan soy margarine

Split pita breads in half. Sprinkle nutritional yeast over bread and dab with margarine. Heat in a toaster oven for a few minutes, until margarine melts. Serve warm.

TOTAL CALORIES PER SERVING: 176   TOTAL FAT AS % OF DAILY VALUE: 9%
PROTEIN: 7 gm   CARBOHYDRATES: 24 gm   FAT: 6 gm
CALCIUM: 50 mg   IRON: 2 mg   SODIUM: 278 mg   DIETARY FIBER: <1 gm

Please Note: If you are on a lowfat diet, we suggest eating fresh fruit or raw vegetables as a snack whenever possible.

SALADS

HEARTY GREEN LEAF SALAD

(Serves 4)

6 leaves green leaf lettuce, washed
2 stalks celery, chopped
1 apple, cored and chopped
1/4 Cup walnuts, chopped or whole

Tear lettuce leaves into bite-size pieces and place them in a large salad bowl. Add chopped celery, apples, and walnuts. Top with your favorite dressing or use the following one.

TOTAL CALORIES PER SERVING: 75   TOTAL FAT AS % OF DAILY VALUE: 6%
PROTEIN: 2 gm   CARBOHYDRATES: 8 gm   FAT: 4 gm
CALCIUM: 20 mg   IRON: 1 mg   SODIUM: 21 mg   DIETARY FIBER: 2 gm

FRUITY SALAD DRESSING

(Serves 4)

1 apple, cored and chopped
1/3 Cup water
1/4 Cup orange juice
1/8 teaspoon cinnamon

Place all the ingredients in a blender and blend at high speed for 2 minutes. Serve over your hearty green leaf salad.

TOTAL CALORIES PER SERVING: 27   TOTAL FAT AS % OF DAILY VALUE: <1%
PROTEIN: <1 gm   CARBOHYDRATES: 7 gm   FAT: <1 gm
CALCIUM: 4 mg   IRON: <1 mg   SODIUM: <1 mg   DIETARY FIBER: <1 gm

GREEN SALAD AND TANGERINE DRESSING

(Serves 4)

6 leaves green leaf lettuce
2 tangerines, peeled and sectioned
1/3 Cup orange juice

Wash lettuce leaves and tear into bite-size pieces. Place lettuce in a large salad bowl. Remove seeds from tangerine sections. Chop half the tangerine sections and place in salad bowl with lettuce. Place the remaining tangerine sections in a blender. Add the orange juice and blend at high speed for 1 minute. Pour tangerine dressing over lettuce and tangerine sections. Toss well. Top salad with the following spicy croutons.

TOTAL CALORIES PER SERVING: 32   TOTAL FAT AS % OF DAILY VALUE: <1%
PROTEIN: 1 gm   CARBOHYDRATES: 8 gm   FAT: <1 gm
CALCIUM: 13 mg   IRON: <1 mg   SODIUM: 4 mg   DIETARY FIBER: 1 gm

SPICY SALAD CROUTONS

(Serves 4)

3 slices of whole wheat bread, cubed
1 Tablespoon olive oil
1/2 teaspoon garlic powder
1/8 teaspoon cayenne pepper
1/2 teaspoon basil

Mix all the ingredients together in a bowl. Spread the mixture on a baking pan. Broil for 3 minutes, stirring once, and remove from oven. Let the croutons cool for a few minutes. Serve over green salad with dressing.

TOTAL CALORIES PER SERVING: 72   TOTAL FAT AS % OF DAILY VALUE: 6%
PROTEIN: 2 gm   CARBOHYDRATES: 8 gm   FAT: 4 gm
CALCIUM: 17 mg   IRON: 1 mg   SODIUM: 91 mg   DIETARY FIBER: 1 gm

COLESLAW

(Serves 8)

Small head green cabbage or 1/2 head small green cabbage plus 1/2 head small red cabbage, shredded
1 small container plain soy yogurt
1 Tablespoon lemon juice
1 teaspoon mustard
Pepper and salt to taste

Mix all the ingredients together in a bowl. If time permits, chill before serving.

TOTAL CALORIES PER SERVING: 25   TOTAL FAT AS % OF DAILY VALUE: 2%
PROTEIN: 2 gm   CARBOHYDRATES: 3 gm   FAT: 1 gm
CALCIUM: 35 mg   IRON: <1 mg   SODIUM: 31 mg   DIETARY FIBER: 2 gm

EASY COLESLAW

(Serves 8-10)

Medium head green cabbage, shredded
2 large carrots, grated
1/2 Cup eggless vegan mayonnaise
1/4 Cup lemon juice
1/2 teaspoon celery seed
Dash of pepper
Salt to taste (optional)

Pour cabbage and carrots into a large bowl. Add the remaining ingredients and toss well. If time permits serve chilled.

TOTAL CALORIES PER SERVING: 68   TOTAL FAT AS % OF DAILY VALUE: 6%
PROTEIN: 2 gm   CARBOHYDRATES: 8 gm   FAT: 4 gm
CALCIUM: 40 mg   IRON: 1 mg   SODIUM: 67 mg   DIETARY FIBER: 3 gm

APPLE CELERY SALAD

(Serves 4)

3 apples, cored and chopped finely
1 stalk celery, chopped finely
1 teaspoon cinnamon
1/2 Cup apple juice

Mix all the ingredients together in a bowl. If time permits, serve chilled.

TOTAL CALORIES PER SERVING: 77   TOTAL FAT AS % OF DAILY VALUE: <1%
PROTEIN: <1 gm   CARBOHYDRATES: 20 gm   FAT: <1 gm
CALCIUM: 13 mg   IRON: <1 mg   SODIUM: 10 mg   DIETARY FIBER: 3 gm

APPLE NUT SALAD

(Serves 4)

3 apples, cored and chopped finely
1/2 Cup walnuts, chopped
1 teaspoon cinnamon
2/3 Cup orange juice

Mix all the ingredients together in a bowl. If time permits, serve chilled.

TOTAL CALORIES PER SERVING: 174   TOTAL FAT AS % OF DAILY VALUE: 14%
PROTEIN: 4 gm   CARBOHYDRATES: 22 gm   FAT: 9 gm
CALCIUM: 20 mg   IRON: 1 mg   SODIUM: <1 mg   DIETARY FIBER: 4 gm

CABBAGE SALAD

(Serves 6)

1/2 head small green cabbage, shredded
2 carrots, grated
1 celery stalk, chopped finely or 1/2 teaspoon celery
   seed
1 clove garlic, minced, or 1/2 teaspoon garlic powder
Pinch of pepper
1/4 Cup each oil and vinegar
1/2 Cup water

Mix all the ingredients together in a bowl. If time permits, serve chilled.

TOTAL CALORIES PER SERVING: 105   TOTAL FAT AS % OF DAILY VALUE: 14%
PROTEIN: 1 gm   CARBOHYDRATES: 6 gm   FAT: 9 gm
CALCIUM: 32 mg   IRON: <1 mg   SODIUM: 23 mg   DIETARY FIBER: 2 gm

STUFFED TOMATO HALVES

(Serves 4)

4 tomatoes
1 small zucchini, grated
1/4 Cup orange juice
1/2 teaspoon garlic powder
1/4 teaspoon oregano
Pepper and salt to taste

Cut a hole in top of each tomato and carefully remove pulp. Place pulp into a bowl and mix in other ingredients. Stuff mixture into tomatoes, and serve.

TOTAL CALORIES PER SERVING: 41   TOTAL FAT AS % OF DAILY VALUE: <1%
PROTEIN: 2 gm   CARBOHYDRATES: 10 gm   FAT: <1 gm
CALCIUM: 21 mg   IRON: 1 mg   SODIUM: 12 mg   DIETARY FIBER: 2 gm

AVOCADO BOATS

(Serves 4)

2 ripe avocados
1/2 ripe tomato, finely chopped
1/3 cucumber, finely chopped
1/4 teaspoon garlic powder
1 teaspoon lemon juice
Pinch cayenne pepper and salt

Carefully cut avocados in half lengthwise and remove seed. Remove avocado pulp from shell and mash in a bowl. Add other ingredients and mix. Put mixture back into avocado shells. Serve with raw carrot and celery sticks.

TOTAL CALORIES PER SERVING: 167   TOTAL FAT AS % OF DAILY VALUE: 25%
PROTEIN: 2 gm   CARBOHYDRATES: 9 gm   FAT: 16 gm
CALCIUM: 15 mg   IRON: 1 mg   SODIUM: 12 mg   DIETARY FIBER: unknown

PASTA FRUIT SALAD

(Serves 4)

2 Cups cooked pasta
2 apples, cored and chopped
2 scallions, finely chopped
5-ounce can water chestnuts, drained and chopped
1 teaspoon tarragon
1/2 Cup raisins

Mix all the ingredients together in a bowl. If time permits, chill before serving.

TOTAL CALORIES PER SERVING: 221   % OF CALORIES FROM FAT: 2%
PROTEIN: 4 gm   CARBOHYDRATES: 52 gm   FAT: 1 gm
CALCIUM: 31 mg   IRON: 1 mg   SODIUM: 7 mg   DIETARY FIBER: 4 gm

EASY PASTA SALAD

(Serves 8)

1 pound pasta, cooked and drained
8-ounce package frozen lima beans, cooked
3 carrots, peeled and finely chopped
1 teaspoon dill weed
1/2 teaspoon salt (optional)
4 Tablespoons eggless vegan mayonnaise

Mix all the ingredients together in a bowl. If time permits, chill before serving.

TOTAL CALORIES PER SERVING: 217   TOTAL FAT AS % OF DAILY VALUE: 5%
PROTEIN: 8 gm   CARBOHYDRATES: 41 gm   FAT: 3 gm
CALCIUM: 27 mg   IRON: 2 mg   SODIUM: 41 mg   DIETARY FIBER: 3 gm

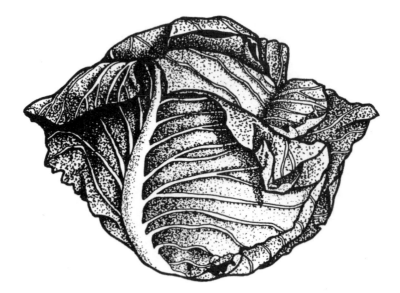

SOUPS

CORN CHOWDER

(Serves 5)

1 Tablespoon oil
1 onion, chopped
2 Cups water
2 stalks celery and 2 carrots, chopped
Two 17-ounce cans vegan creamed corn
1 Cup soy milk
1 potato, chopped
1-1/2 teaspoons garlic powder
1/4 teaspoon nutmeg
Salt and pepper to taste

Sauté onion in oil over medium-high heat until soft. Add water and
chopped celery and carrots. Cook 10 minutes. Add creamed corn,
soy milk, chopped potato, and spices. Continue cooking for another 10
minutes. Serve hot.

TOTAL CALORIES PER SERVING: 166   TOTAL FAT AS % OF DAILY VALUE: 8%
PROTEIN: 5 gm   CARBOHYDRATES: 30 gm   FAT: 5 gm
CALCIUM: 40 mg   IRON: 1 mg   SODIUM: 315 mg   DIETARY FIBER: 4 gm

QUICK CABBAGE SOUP

(Serves 2)

2 Cups Chinese cabbage or green cabbage, shredded
2 teaspoons oil
3 Cups water
1 vegetable bouillon cube

Sauté cabbage in oil for 2 minutes over medium-high heat. Add water and bouillon cube. Continue cooking over medium heat for 8 minutes. Serve hot.

TOTAL CALORIES PER SERVING: 54   TOTAL FAT AS % OF DAILY VALUE: 8%
PROTEIN: 1 gm   CARBOHYDRATES: 2 gm   FAT: 5 gm
CALCIUM: 75 mg   IRON: 1 mg   SODIUM: 386 mg   DIETARY FIBER: 3 gm

LEMON RICE SOUP

(Serves 6-8)

1 small onion or 3 scallions, chopped
1/2 head small cabbage, shredded
1/2 teaspoon garlic powder
1/8 teaspoon black pepper
1/8 teaspoon turmeric
2 Tablespoons oil
3 Cups pre-cooked rice
8 Cups water or vegetable broth
1/4 Cup lemon juice
1 Cup nutritional yeast
1 Tablespoon tamari or soy sauce

Sauté onion or scallions, cabbage, and spices in oil for 5-8 minutes. Add rice, water or broth, lemon juice, yeast, and tamari or soy sauce. Simmer for another 10 minutes. Serve hot.

Variation: Instead of cabbage use 2 cups chopped fresh kale.

TOTAL CALORIES PER SERVING: 232   TOTAL FAT AS % OF DAILY VALUE: 8%
PROTEIN: 11 gm   CARBOHYDRATES: 37 gm   FAT: 5 gm
CALCIUM: 82 mg   IRON: 5 mg   SODIUM: 212 mg   DIETARY FIBER: 2 gm

QUICK PEA SOUP

(Serves 4)

1 small onion, minced
1 Tablespoon oil
Salt and pepper to taste
Two 10-ounce boxes of frozen peas
1 Cup soy milk
1 Cup pre-cooked rice or barley (optional)

Sauté onion in oil over medium-high heat for 3 minutes. Add salt and pepper, and peas. Cook 5 minutes longer, stirring occasionally. Pour mixture into a blender. Add soy milk and blend until creamy. Pour blended mixture back into a pot. Reheat a few minutes, adding pre-cooked rice or barley if desired.

TOTAL CALORIES PER SERVING: 162   TOTAL FAT AS % OF DAILY VALUE: 9%
PROTEIN: 8 gm   CARBOHYDRATES: 21 gm   FAT: 6 gm
CALCIUM: 53 mg   IRON: 2 mg   SODIUM: 130 mg   DIETARY FIBER: 6 gm

CREAM OF CELERY SOUP

(Serves 3)

6 stalks of celery, chopped
1 small onion, chopped finely
1 Tablespoon oil
1/8 teaspoon pepper
1/4 teaspoon garlic powder
1-1/2 Cups soy milk
1/2 Cup water

Sauté celery and onion in oil until onion is clear. Turn off heat. Pour mixture into a blender. Add remaining ingredients. Blend until creamy. Pour mixture back into a pot. Reheat for a few minutes and serve hot.

TOTAL CALORIES PER SERVING: 138   TOTAL FAT AS % OF DAILY VALUE: 12%
PROTEIN: 6 gm   CARBOHYDRATES: 12 gm   FAT: 8 gm
CALCIUM: 77 mg   IRON: 1 mg   SODIUM: 136 mg   DIETARY FIBER: 1 gm

CREAMY CAULIFLOWER SOUP

(Serves 4)

1 Cup water
1 head cauliflower, chopped
2 Cups water
1/2 Cup shredded coconut
1/2 teaspoon cinnamon
1/4 teaspoon nutmeg

Steam chopped cauliflower in 1 cup water over medium-high heat for about 12 minutes, until tender. Drain. Place half of the steamed cauliflower and coconut in a blender. Add 1 Cup of water to blender and cream mixture. Pour blended mixture back into a pot. Blend the remaining steamed cauliflower and spices with another cup of water. Add this mixture to the pot also. Reheat mixture over medium heat for 8 minutes and serve hot.

TOTAL CALORIES PER SERVING: 69   TOTAL FAT AS % OF DAILY VALUE: 9%
PROTEIN: 1 gm   CARBOHYDRATES: 3 gm   FAT: 6 gm
CALCIUM: 13 mg   IRON: 1 mg   SODIUM: 7 mg   DIETARY FIBER: 2 gm

COLD TOMATO SOUP

(Serves 4)

6 Cups cold no salt added tomato juice
1 cucumber, finely chopped
2 scallions, finely chopped

2 stalks celery, finely chopped
2 ripe tomatoes, chopped
1/4 teaspoon cayenne pepper
1/2 teaspoon each onion powder and garlic powder
1 teaspoon basil

Mix all the ingredients together and serve chilled.

TOTAL CALORIES PER SERVING: 85   TOTAL FAT AS % OF DAILY VALUE: <1%
PROTEIN: 4 gm   CARBOHYDRATES: 21 gm   FAT: <1 gm
CALCIUM: 58 mg   IRON: 3 mg   SODIUM: 68 mg   DIETARY FIBER: 1 gm

CREAMY LENTIL SOUP

(Serves 4)

3 carrots, chopped
1 large onion, chopped
2 Tablespoons oil
1-1/2 Cups red lentils
4 Cups water
1 Tablespoon marjoram
Salt and pepper to taste
1 Cup water
Slices of lemon

Sauté carrots and onion in oil over medium-high heat until onions are clear. Add remaining ingredients (except 1 cup water and lemon slices) and bring to a boil. Lower heat, but continue cooking over medium-high heat for 20 minutes. Pour mixture into a blender. Blend until creamy. Return mixture to a pot and add 1 cup of water. Reheat for a few minutes, until hot. Serve soup garnished with lemon slices.

TOTAL CALORIES PER SERVING: 289   TOTAL FAT AS % OF DAILY VALUE: 12%
PROTEIN: 16 gm   CARBOHYDRATES: 42 gm   FAT: 8 gm
CALCIUM: 54 mg   IRON: 6 mg   SODIUM: 23 mg   DIETARY FIBER: 8 gm

ZUCCHINI/MUSHROOM SOUP

(Serves 6)

1 small onion, chopped
1 Tablespoon oil
3 or 4 medium zucchini, chopped
1/2 pound mushrooms, chopped
6 Cups water
1/2 Cup rolled oats
1/2 teaspoon salt (optional)
2 Tablespoons parsley, finely chopped

Sauté onion in oil until clear. Add zucchini and mushrooms. Sauté 5 minutes longer. Add water, oats, and seasonings. Simmer 12 minutes. Pour mixture into a blender. Blend until creamy. Return mixture to a pot and reheat. Serve hot.

TOTAL CALORIES PER SERVING: 84   TOTAL FAT AS % OF DAILY VALUE: 5%
PROTEIN: 3 gm   CARBOHYDRATES: 12 gm   FAT: 3 gm
CALCIUM: 33 mg   IRON: 1 mg   SODIUM: 5 mg   DIETARY FIBER: 3 gm

SIDE DISHES

BROCCOLI SAUTÉ

(Serves 4)

1 pound broccoli (about 3 stalks), chopped
1 onion, chopped
1-1/2 teaspoons oil
1/2 Cup water
1 Tablespoon caraway seeds

Sauté ingredients in a large frying pan over medium-high heat for 10 minutes.

TOTAL CALORIES PER SERVING: 54   TOTAL FAT AS % OF DAILY VALUE: 3%
PROTEIN: 4 gm   CARBOHYDRATES: 8 gm   FAT: 2 gm
CALCIUM: 64 mg   IRON: 1 mg   SODIUM: 27 mg   DIETARY FIBER: 3 gm

CORN FRITTERS

(Serves 3-4)

1/2 Cup each cornmeal and pre-cooked corn kernels
2/3 Cup whole wheat pastry or unbleached white flour
1/4 Cup cornstarch
2 Tablespoons tamari or soy sauce
2/3 Cup soy milk or water

Combine all the ingredients together, mixing well. Form 8 fritters and fry in a lightly oiled pan over medium-high heat until brown on both sides.

TOTAL CALORIES PER SERVING: 273   TOTAL FAT AS % OF DAILY VALUE: 5%
PROTEIN: 9 gm   CARBOHYDRATES: 56 gm   FAT: 3 gm
CALCIUM: 34 mg   IRON: 2 mg   SODIUM: 804 mg   DIETARY FIBER: 3 gm

CAULIFLOWER AND CARROTS

(Serves 5)

1 head cauliflower, chopped
2-3 carrots, thinly sliced
1-1/2 teaspoons oil
1/3 Cup water
Juice from 1/2 lemon
1/2 teaspoon dry mustard powder
1/4 teaspoon tarragon
Salt and pepper to taste

Steam cauliflower and carrots over boiling water for 10 minutes. Remove from heat. Add steamed cauliflower and carrots to remaining ingredients in a wok or skillet. Stir-fry over medium-high heat for 5-10 minutes.

TOTAL CALORIES PER SERVING: 36   TOTAL FAT AS % OF DAILY VALUE: 3%
PROTEIN: 1 gm   CARBOHYDRATES: 6 gm   FAT: 2 gm
CALCIUM: 19 mg   IRON: <1 mg   SODIUM: 16 mg   DIETARY FIBER: 3 gm

STEAMED CAULIFLOWER WITH DILL SAUCE

(Serves 6)

1 head cauliflower, broken into flowerets
3 Tablespoons vegan soy margarine
1 teaspoon dill weed
1 Tablespoon nutritional yeast
1/3 Cup water

Steam cauliflower over boiling water until tender. Meanwhile, melt margarine in a separate pan. Stir in dill weed, yeast, and water. Add steamed cauliflower and mix well before serving.

TOTAL CALORIES PER SERVING: 58   TOTAL FAT AS % OF DAILY VALUE: 9%
PROTEIN: 1 gm   CARBOHYDRATES: 2 gm   FAT: 6 gm
CALCIUM: 11 mg   IRON: <1 mg   SODIUM: 69 mg   DIETARY FIBER: 2 gm

SWEET ORANGE RICE

(Serves 3-4)

1 Cup basmati rice
5 Tablespoons orange juice concentrate
2-1/2 Cups water
1/2 teaspoon cinnamon

Heat all the ingredients in a pot over high heat until the water begins to boil. Lower heat and simmer 15-20 minutes, until rice is done.

TOTAL CALORIES PER SERVING: 307   TOTAL FAT AS % OF DAILY VALUE: <1%
PROTEIN: 5 gm   CARBOHYDRATES: 70 gm   FAT: <1 gm
CALCIUM: 37 mg   IRON: 2 mg   SODIUM: 7.5 mg   DIETARY FIBER: 0.8 gm

SEASONED RICE

(Serves 4-5)

1 Cup basmati rice
2 Tablespoons vegan soy margarine
2/3 Cup water
2 Tablespoons nutritional yeast
Salt to taste
1/2 teaspoon garlic powder
1 teaspoon basil
10-ounce box frozen corn and/or peas (optional)

Cook rice in 3 cups water until done. Melt margarine in pan. Add remaining ingredients except rice. Heat 5 minutes. Add cooked rice and heat 2 minutes.

TOTAL CALORIES PER SERVING: 227   TOTAL FAT AS % OF DAILY VALUE: 8%
PROTEIN: 5 gm   CARBOHYDRATES: 39 gm   FAT: 5 gm
CALCIUM: 26 mg   IRON: 2 mg   SODIUM: 63 mg   DIETARY FIBER: <1 gm

FRIED RICE

(Serves 4)

1 Cup basmati rice
3 Cups water
2 teaspoons oil
2 stalks celery, finely chopped
1 large green pepper, finely chopped
2 scallions, finely chopped
1 Tablespoon fresh ginger, grated
3 Tablespoons soy sauce or tamari

Cook rice in water until done. When rice is cooked, add remaining ingredients and stir-fry over medium heat for 5 minutes.

TOTAL CALORIES PER SERVING: 206   TOTAL FAT AS % OF DAILY VALUE: 5%
PROTEIN: 4 gm   CARBOHYDRATES: 41 gm   FAT: 3 gm
CALCIUM: 33 mg   IRON: 2 mg   SODIUM: 795 mg   DIETARY FIBER: 1 gm

LEMONY RICE

(Serves 4)

1-1/2 Cups basmati rice
4 Cups water
1/2 lemon

Bring water to a boil. Add rice. Squeeze lemon juice into pot, then put whole rind in the pot also. Cook until rice is done. Remove rind before serving.

TOTAL CALORIES PER SERVING: 254   TOTAL FAT AS % OF DAILY VALUE: <1%
PROTEIN: 5 gm   CARBOHYDRATES: 57 gm   FAT: <1 gm
CALCIUM: 26 mg   IRON: 2 mg   SODIUM: 7 mg   DIETARY FIBER: <1 gm

ZUCCHINI PANCAKES

(Serves 4-5)

1 medium zucchini
1 small onion
1/2 Cup water
1 Cup whole wheat pastry flour
1/2 teaspoon garlic powder
1 Tablespoon parsley flakes
1 teaspoon tamari or soy sauce
2 teaspoons oil

Blend zucchini, onion, and water in a food processor. Pour into a bowl and add flour, garlic, parsley, and soy sauce. Form 10 small pancakes and fry in an oiled pan over medium heat. Brown both sides.

TOTAL CALORIES PER SERVING: 139   TOTAL FAT AS % OF DAILY VALUE: 5%
PROTEIN: 5 gm   CARBOHYDRATES: 25 gm   FAT: 3 gm
CALCIUM: 29 mg   IRON: 1 mg   SODIUM: 89 mg   DIETARY FIBER: 4 gm

STEAMED SQUASH

(Serves 4)

2 yellow squash, thinly sliced
2 zucchini, thinly sliced
1 Tablespoon soy sauce or tamari
1 teaspoon each nutritional yeast and dill weed

Steam yellow squash and zucchini over water for 10-15 minutes (depending on how tender you prefer your vegetables). Remove squash and place in a dish. Sprinkle with soy sauce or tamari, nutritional yeast, and dill weed.

Variation: Stir in 1 cup croutons or vegan Chinese dry noodles before serving.

TOTAL CALORIES PER SERVING: 50   TOTAL FAT AS % OF DAILY VALUE: <1%
PROTEIN: 3 gm   CARBOHYDRATES: 11 gm   FAT: <1 gm
CALCIUM: 48 mg   IRON: 1 mg   SODIUM: 264 mg   DIETARY FIBER: 4 gm

RED HOT ZUCCHINI

(Serves 3)

2 large zucchini, thinly sliced
2 small red hot peppers, minced
2 teaspoons oil

Stir-fry ingredients over medium-high heat for 5 minutes. Lower heat
and cover pan. Continue to heat for 5 more minutes, stirring occasionally. Add a little bit of soy sauce for taste if desired.

TOTAL CALORIES PER SERVING: 66   TOTAL FAT AS % OF DAILY VALUE: 5%
PROTEIN: 2 gm   CARBOHYDRATES: 9 gm   FAT: 3 gm
CALCIUM: 34 mg   IRON: 1 mg   SODIUM: 5 mg   DIETARY FIBER: 3 gm

ZUCCHINI, PEPPER, AND CORN

(Serves 4)

1 pound zucchini, chopped
1 small onion, chopped
1 large green pepper, chopped
1 Cup fresh or frozen corn
1/2 teaspoon each parsley flakes and onion powder
1/4 teaspoon pepper
2 teaspoons oil or 1/3 Cup water

Sauté all the ingredients until vegetables are tender.

TOTAL CALORIES PER SERVING: 68   TOTAL FAT AS % OF DAILY VALUE: 2%
PROTEIN: 3 gm   CARBOHYDRATES: 15 gm   FAT: 1 gm
CALCIUM: 31 mg   IRON: 1 mg   SODIUM: 136 mg   DIETARY FIBER: 4 gm

TOMATO/ZUCCHINI STIR-FRY

(Serves 5)

3 medium zucchini, thinly sliced
1 small onion, minced
3 medium tomatoes, chopped
1 Tablespoon garlic powder
2 Tablespoons basil
1/4 Cup nutritional yeast
Salt to taste
1 Tablespoon oil
1/2 Cup water

Stir-fry all the ingredients over medium-high heat until zucchini is tender.

TOTAL CALORIES PER SERVING: 89   TOTAL FAT AS % OF DAILY VALUE: 5%
PROTEIN: 5 gm   CARBOHYDRATES: 13 gm   FAT: 3 gm
CALCIUM: 50 mg   IRON: 2 mg   SODIUM: 18 mg   DIETARY FIBER: 3 gm

CELERY SAUTÉ

(Serves 2)

5 stalks celery, chopped
1-1/2 teaspoons oil
1/3 Cup water
1 teaspoon tarragon
1 teaspoon soy sauce or tamari

Sauté ingredients over medium-high heat for 3-5 minutes.

Variation: Use chopped bok choy instead of celery.

TOTAL CALORIES PER SERVING: 47   TOTAL FAT AS % OF DAILY VALUE: 5%
PROTEIN: 1 gm   CARBOHYDRATES: 4 gm   FAT: 3 gm
CALCIUM: 37 mg   IRON: <1 mg   SODIUM: 259 mg   DIETARY FIBER: 2 gm

VEGETABLE MEDLEY

(Serves 4)

2 carrots, peeled and chopped
2 stalks celery and 2 yellow squash, chopped
1 onion, chopped
1/2 pound mushrooms, chopped
1-1/2 Tablespoons oil
10-ounce box frozen peas
1 Tablespoon basil

Stir-fry carrots, celery, squash, onion, and mushrooms in oil for 5 minutes over medium-high heat. Add peas and basil. Heat for 5 minutes longer and serve.

TOTAL CALORIES PER SERVING: 163   TOTAL FAT AS % OF DAILY VALUE: 9%
PROTEIN: 7 gm   CARBOHYDRATES: 24 gm   FAT: 6 gm
CALCIUM: 65 mg   IRON: 3 mg   SODIUM: 95 mg   DIETARY FIBER: 8 gm

CABBAGE, RAISINS, AND COCONUT

(Serves 4-5)

1 small cabbage, chopped
1-1/2 Tablespoons oil
1 Cup raisins
1/3 Cup shredded unsweetened coconut

1 teaspoon cinnamon

Heat ingredients over medium-high heat in covered pan, stirring occasionally, for about 12 minutes or until cabbage is tender.

TOTAL CALORIES PER SERVING: 235   TOTAL FAT AS % OF DAILY VALUE: 15%
PROTEIN: 3 gm   CARBOHYDRATES: 40 gm   FAT: 10 gm
CALCIUM: 73 mg   IRON: 2 mg   SODIUM: 26 mg   DIETARY FIBER: 7 gm

CABBAGE/SPROUT SAUTÉ

(Serves 6)

1/2 head cabbage, chopped
1 stalk broccoli, chopped
Small onion, minced
1 Tablespoon oil
1/2 Cup water
1 teaspoon garlic powder
1 Tablespoon caraway seeds
1 pound mung bean sprouts

Sauté all the ingredients, except the sprouts and soy sauce, for 5 minutes. Add sprouts and sauté for 5 minutes longer. Add soy sauce, if desired.

TOTAL CALORIES PER SERVING: 66   TOTAL FAT AS % OF DAILY VALUE: 5%
PROTEIN: 4 gm   CARBOHYDRATES: 10 gm   FAT: 3 gm
CALCIUM: 48 mg   IRON: 1 mg   SODIUM: 19 mg   DIETARY FIBER: 2 gm

SWEET SAUTÉED RED CABBAGE

(Serves 4)

1/2 red cabbage, shredded
1 apple, chopped

Small onion, chopped
1/2 Cup water
1/2 Cup raisins
1/2 teaspoon cinnamon

Use a non-stick pan, if possible, and heat ingredients, stirring occasion-ally, over medium-high heat for 10 minutes.

TOTAL CALORIES PER SERVING: 106   TOTAL FAT AS % OF DAILY VALUE: <1%
PROTEIN: 2 gm   CARBOHYDRATES: 27 gm   FAT: <1 gm
CALCIUM: 50 mg   IRON: 1 mg   SODIUM: 16 mg   DIETARY FIBER: 5 gm

CREAMED MUSHROOMS AND SQUASH

(Serves 6)

1 pound mushrooms, sliced
2 small zucchini or yellow squash, finely chopped
Small onion, chopped
1 teaspoon dill weed
Salt and pepper to taste
1 Tablespoon oil
1/2 Cup water
1-1/2 Cups soy milk
2 Tablespoons unbleached white flour or whole wheat
      pastry flour
2 Tablespoons nutritional yeast (optional)

Stir-fry mushrooms, zucchini or yellow squash, onion, and spices in oil and water over medium-high heat for 10 minutes until squash is tender. Add soy milk, flour, and nutritional yeast. Stir until sauce is thick.

TOTAL CALORIES PER SERVING: 106   TOTAL FAT AS % OF DAILY VALUE: 8%
PROTEIN: 5 gm   CARBOHYDRATES: 13 gm   FAT: 5 gm
CALCIUM: 44 mg   IRON: 2 mg   SODIUM: 38 mg   DIETARY FIBER: 3 gm

STUFFED MUSHROOMS

(Serves 2-3)

10 large mushrooms
1/3 pound yellow squash
1/3 small onion
1/2 carrot
1/8 teaspoon each garlic powder and pepper
1 Tablespoon oil

Remove stems from mushrooms. Chop stems, squash, and onion. Peel and grate carrot. Sauté ingredients, except mushroom caps, over medium-high heat for 10 minutes, until squash is tender. Stuff mushroom caps with mixture. Heat stuffed mushrooms in oiled pan for 5 minutes over medium heat.

TOTAL CALORIES PER SERVING: 121   TOTAL FAT AS % OF DAILY VALUE: 12%
PROTEIN: 4 gm   CARBOHYDRATES: 12 gm   FAT: 8 gm
CALCIUM: 30 mg   IRON: 2 mg   SODIUM: 14 mg   DIETARY FIBER: 3 gm

SAUTÉED MUSHROOMS WITH FRESH PARSLEY

(Serves 4)

1 pound mushrooms
1 Tablespoon oil
1/2 Cup water
1-1/2 teaspoons garlic powder
1 Cup fresh parsley, chopped

Sauté mushrooms in oil and water with garlic powder for 5 minutes. Lower heat and add chopped parsley. Sauté another 5 minutes.

TOTAL CALORIES PER SERVING: 64   TOTAL FAT AS % OF DAILY VALUE: 6%
PROTEIN: 3 gm   CARBOHYDRATES: 6 gm   FAT: 4 gm
CALCIUM: 25 mg   IRON: 2 mg   SODIUM: 11 mg   DIETARY FIBER: 3 gm

CURRIED CELERY AND MUSHROOMS

(Serves 4)

3 stalks celery, chopped
1 pound mushrooms, sliced
1 teaspoon oil
2 Tablespoons water
2 teaspoons curry powder
1/2 teaspoon garlic powder
Salt and pepper to taste

Sauté ingredients in a large frying pan over medium-high heat for 10 minutes.

TOTAL CALORIES PER SERVING: 44   TOTAL FAT AS % OF DAILY VALUE: 3%
PROTEIN: 3 gm   CARBOHYDRATES: 7 gm   FAT: 2 gm
CALCIUM: 18 mg   IRON: 2 mg   SODIUM: 306 mg   DIETARY FIBER: 3 gm

GOLDEN CHUTNEY

(Serves 6)

1 Cup dried figs, chopped
1 apple, chopped
1/2 lemon with seeds removed, chopped (including peel)
1/2 Cup molasses
1/4 Cup vinegar
1 teaspoon allspice
1/2 teaspoon cinnamon

Place ingredients in pot. Bring to a boil, then simmer for 25 minutes.

TOTAL CALORIES PER SERVING: 142   TOTAL FAT AS % OF DAILY VALUE: <1%
PROTEIN: 1 gm   CARBOHYDRATES: 37 gm   FAT: <1 gm
CALCIUM: 117 mg   IRON: 2 mg   SODIUM: 12 mg   DIETARY FIBER: 3 gm

BOK CHOY STIR-FRY

(Serves 4)

2 bunches bok choy
2 teaspoons oil
1/2 teaspoon garlic powder
1 Tablespoon soy sauce
2 teaspoons sesame oil

Separate bok choy leaves and stems from one another, keeping stems. Chop stems. Heat oil over medium-high heat in a wok or large frying pan. Add bok choy stems and leaves and garlic powder. Stir-fry for 5 minutes. Lower heat and add soy sauce and sesame oil. Stir for 1 minute and serve.

TOTAL CALORIES PER SERVING: 72   TOTAL FAT AS % OF DAILY VALUE: 8%
PROTEIN: 4 gm   CARBOHYDRATES: 5 gm   FAT: 5 gm
CALCIUM: 240 mg   IRON: 2 mg   SODIUM: 407 mg   DIETARY FIBER: unknown

BOK CHOY AND CARROTS

(Serves 4)

1 pound bok choy, chopped
1 carrot, peeled and very thinly sliced
1 teaspoon tarragon
2 teaspoons soy sauce or tamari
1-1/2 teaspoons oil
1/3 Cup water

Sauté ingredients in oil and water over medium heat for 8-10 minutes.

TOTAL CALORIES PER SERVING: 39   TOTAL FAT AS % OF DAILY VALUE: 3%
PROTEIN: 2 gm   CARBOHYDRATES: 5 gm   FAT: 2 gm
CALCIUM: 125 mg   IRON: 1 mg   SODIUM: 253 mg   DIETARY FIBER: unknown

BOK CHOY AND APPLE

(Serves 4)

1 pound bok choy, chopped
1-1/2 teaspoons oil
1/3 Cup water
1 apple, chopped
1 teaspoon ginger powder

Stir-fry ingredients over medium heat for 5 minutes.

TOTAL CALORIES PER SERVING: 52   TOTAL FAT AS % OF DAILY VALUE: 3%
PROTEIN: 2 gm   CARBOHYDRATES: 8 gm   FAT: 2 gm
CALCIUM: 122 mg   IRON: 1 mg   SODIUM: 75 mg   DIETARY FIBER: unknown

BREADED OKRA

(Serves 3)

10-ounce box frozen okra (or fresh)
1/2 Cup water
1 teaspoon soy sauce or tamari
Pepper to taste
1/4 Cup corn meal
1 Tablespoon oil

Cook okra in water for 8 minutes. Remove from heat and drain. Sprinkle with soy sauce and pepper. Dredge okra in corn meal. Fry in oil over medium-high heat until brown on all sides (a few minutes).

TOTAL CALORIES PER SERVING: 116   TOTAL FAT AS % OF DAILY VALUE: 8%
PROTEIN: 3 gm   CARBOHYDRATES: 16 gm   FAT: 5 gm
CALCIUM: 87mg   IRON: 1 mg   SODIUM: 117 mg   DIETARY FIBER: unknown

EGGPLANT/OKRA DISH

(Serves 5)

Small eggplant, peeled and cubed
1 pound fresh okra, chopped
2 stalks celery, chopped
1-1/2 teaspoons oil
8-ounce can tomato sauce
1/2 teaspoon basil
Pepper to taste

Sauté eggplant, okra, and celery in oil for 2 minutes. Add sauce and spices. Heat for 5 minutes longer, stirring occasionally.

TOTAL CALORIES PER SERVING: 96   TOTAL FAT AS % OF DAILY VALUE: 8%
PROTEIN: 3 gm   CARBOHYDRATES: 13 gm   FAT: 5 gm
CALCIUM: 100 mg   IRON: 1 mg   SODIUM: 314 mg   DIETARY FIBER: unknown

STUFFED TOMATOES WITH MINTED RICE

(Serves 4)

1/2 Cup basmati rice
1-1/2 Cups water
4 ripe tomatoes
2 teaspoons dried mint
1/4 teaspoon salt

Cook rice in boiling water until done. Carefully remove core and pulp from tomatoes. Then bake tomatoes at 400 degrees for 10 minutes.

Add mint and salt to cooked rice, mixing well. Stuff tomatoes with rice mixture. Broil for 10 minutes and serve.

TOTAL CALORIES PER SERVING: 107   TOTAL FAT AS % OF DAILY VALUE: <1%
PROTEIN: 3 gm   CARBOHYDRATES: 24 gm   FAT: <1 gm
CALCIUM: 17 mg   IRON: 1 mg   SODIUM: 150 mg   DIETARY FIBER: 2 gm

BROILED HERBED TOMATOES

(Serves 3)

3 tomatoes, cut in half
1 Tablespoon vegan soy margarine
1 teaspoon basil
2 Tablespoons nutritional yeast
Dash of salt and pepper

Place margarine, basil, yeast, salt, and pepper on top of tomatoes. Broil for 4 minutes, until tops are slightly brown.

TOTAL CALORIES PER SERVING: 71   TOTAL FAT AS % OF DAILY VALUE: 6%
PROTEIN: 3 gm   CARBOHYDRATES: 7 gm   FAT: 4 gm
CALCIUM: 21 mg   IRON: 2 mg   SODIUM: 60 mg   DIETARY FIBER: 2 gm

ORIENTAL-STYLE GREEN BEANS

(Serves 5)

1-1/2 pounds fresh green beans, snapped in half
2 teaspoons oil
3 cloves garlic, minced
1 teaspoon ginger powder

Stir-fry ingredients for 10 minutes over medium-high heat. Lower heat and if desired, add 1 Tablespoon sesame oil. Heat 2 more minutes until beans are tender, yet firm.

Variation: Add 1/4 cup pine nuts or almond slivers during last two minutes of heating.

TOTAL CALORIES PER SERVING: 54   TOTAL FAT AS % OF DAILY VALUE: 3%
PROTEIN: 2 gm   CARBOHYDRATES: 9 gm   FAT: 2 gm
CALCIUM: 64 mg   IRON: 1 mg   SODIUM: 19 mg   DIETARY FIBER: 4 gm

MINTED GREEN BEANS AND BEETS

(Serves 4)

1 pound fresh green beans, snapped in half
4 fresh beets, peeled and thinly sliced
1/2 teaspoon dried mint
1 Cup water

Cook ingredients for 20 minutes over medium-high heat in covered pot.

TOTAL CALORIES PER SERVING: 45   TOTAL FAT AS % OF DAILY VALUE: <1%
PROTEIN: 2 gm   CARBOHYDRATES: 10 gm   FAT: <1 gm
CALCIUM: 57 mg   IRON: 1 mg   SODIUM: 40 mg   DIETARY FIBER: unknown

SWEET AND SOUR CARROTS

(Serves 4)

1 pound carrots, thinly sliced
1 Tablespoon vinegar
2 Tablespoons water
2 Tablespoons molasses
1/4 teaspoon nutmeg
1/2 Cup raisins

Heat all the ingredients in a covered pan over medium heat, stirring occasionally, for 10 minutes.

TOTAL CALORIES PER SERVING: 135   TOTAL FAT AS % OF DAILY VALUE: <1%
PROTEIN: 2 gm   CARBOHYDRATES: 34 gm   FAT: <1 gm
CALCIUM: 70 mg   IRON: 2 mg   SODIUM: 46 mg   DIETARY FIBER: 5 gm

SESAME CARROTS WITH DILL WEED

(Serves 4)

6 carrots, peeled and thinly sliced
2 Cups water
1 teaspoon dill weed
2 teaspoons sesame oil
2 teaspoons sesame seeds (optional)

Heat carrots in water for approximately 10 minutes over a medium-high heat in a large uncovered frying pan, until most of the water evaporates. Carrots will be slightly tender. Reduce heat to low. Add dill weed, sesame oil, and sesame seeds if desired. Heat 2 minutes longer and serve.

TOTAL CALORIES PER SERVING: 67   TOTAL FAT AS % OF DAILY VALUE: 3%
PROTEIN: 1 gm   CARBOHYDRATES: 11 gm   FAT: 2 gm
CALCIUM: 29 mg   IRON: 1 mg   SODIUM: 38 mg   DIETARY FIBER: 3 gm

CREAMED SPINACH

(Serves 4)

10-ounce box frozen chopped spinach
1/2 Cup water
1 Cup soy milk

1 Tablespoon cornstarch
1/4 teaspoon nutmeg
1/2 teaspoon garlic powder
1 teaspoon soy sauce

Cook spinach in water over medium heat for 15 minutes. Add remaining ingredients and simmer over medium-low heat for 3 minutes longer, stirring often.

TOTAL CALORIES PER SERVING: 66   TOTAL FAT AS % OF DAILY VALUE: 3%
PROTEIN: 5 gm   CARBOHYDRATES: 9 gm   FAT: 2 gm
CALCIUM: 121 mg   IRON: 1 mg   SODIUM: 177 mg   DIETARY FIBER: 2 gm

SAUTÉED SPINACH WITH WATER CHESTNUTS

(Serves 3)

10-ounce bag fresh spinach, washed and chopped
1 Tablespoon oil
1/3 Cup water
2 cloves garlic, minced
1/2 teaspoon cumin
1/8 teaspoon cayenne pepper
1 Tablespoon lemon juice
4 ounces water chestnuts, thinly sliced

Sauté all the ingredients over medium-high heat for 5 minutes.

TOTAL CALORIES PER SERVING: 104   TOTAL FAT AS % OF DAILY VALUE: 8%
PROTEIN: 3 gm   CARBOHYDRATES: 13 gm   FAT: 5 gm
CALCIUM: 98 mg   IRON: 3 mg   SODIUM: 77 mg   DIETARY FIBER: 2 gm

CREAMED POTATOES, ONIONS, AND PEAS

(Serves 6-8)

2 pounds very small red or white potatoes, sliced thinly
3 Tablespoons vegan soy margarine
6 Tablespoons unbleached white flour or whole wheat
    pastry flour
1-1/2 Cups lowfat soy milk
1-1/4 Cups water
2 teaspoons mustard
Two 10-ounce boxes frozen pearl onions
10-ounce box frozen peas
Minced fresh parsley for garnish

Cook potatoes in boiling water for 15-20 minutes, until tender.

Meanwhile, melt margarine in a pan. Add flour, soy milk, and water. Stir until mixture thickens, about 2 minutes. Add mustard, salt, and pepper to taste. Add onions and peas and heat for 5 minutes longer, stirring often. Add potatoes and garnish with parsley.

TOTAL CALORIES PER SERVING: 299   TOTAL FAT AS % OF DAILY VALUE: 11%
PROTEIN: 9 gm   CARBOHYDRATES: 54 gm   FAT: 7 gm
CALCIUM: 76 mg   IRON: 2 mg   SODIUM: 139 mg   DIETARY FIBER: 5 gm

STEAMED POTATOES WITH SAUTÉED ONIONS

(Serves 4)

4 potatoes, peeled and thinly sliced
1 Tablespoon oil or 1/4 Cup water
1 large onion, chopped
1 teaspoon tarragon
1/4 teaspoon pepper

Steam sliced potatoes over boiling water until tender.

Sauté onion and spices in a separate pot in oil or water over medium heat, until onions are transparent. Serve onions over potatoes.

TOTAL CALORIES PER SERVING: 157   TOTAL FAT AS % OF DAILY VALUE: 6%
PROTEIN: 3 gm   CARBOHYDRATES: 29 gm   FAT: 4 gm
CALCIUM: 19 mg   IRON: 1 mg   SODIUM: 8 mg   DIETARY FIBER: 3 gm

SAUTÉED COLLARDS AND TOMATOES

(Serves 4)

1 teaspoon oil
1 pound collards, chopped into bite-size pieces
2 ripe tomatoes, chopped
2 teaspoons lemon juice
1/2 teaspoon garlic powder
1/4 teaspoon mustard powder

Sauté all the ingredients together over medium-high heat for 3-5 minutes. Serve hot.

TOTAL CALORIES PER SERVING: 38   TOTAL FAT AS % OF DAILY VALUE: 3%
PROTEIN: 2 gm   CARBOHYDRATES: 6 gm   FAT: 2 gm
CALCIUM: 94 mg   IRON: 1 mg   SODIUM: 27 mg   DIETARY FIBER: 3 gm

MAIN DISHES

BROCCOLI AND CASHEWS OVER MILLET

(Serves 5)

2 Cups millet
6 Cups water
2 Tablespoons oil
2 teaspoons mustard seed
1 large bunch broccoli, chopped
1 onion, chopped
1/2 Cup water
1/2 Cup cashews, chopped
1 Tablespoon soy sauce

Cook millet in 6 cups of water in a covered pot over a medium-high heat for 15-20 minutes. The millet will become soft.

While the millet is cooking, heat oil in a large pan. Add mustard seeds and cover pan. As the seeds fry they will begin to pop (like popcorn). When you no longer hear any seeds popping (a minute or so), add the broccoli, onion, water, cashews, and soy sauce. Sauté ingredients about 15 minutes until broccoli is tender. Serve sautéed mixture over the cooked millet.

TOTAL CALORIES PER SERVING: 307   TOTAL FAT AS % OF DAILY VALUE: 20%
PROTEIN: 9 gm   CARBOHYDRATES: 41 gm   FAT: 13 gm
CALCIUM: 66 mg   IRON: 4 mg   SODIUM: 312 mg   DIETARY FIBER: 9 gm

MEXICAN-STYLE CHICKPEAS

(Serves 3)

19-ounce can cooked chickpeas (garbanzo beans), drained (or 2 Cups pre-cooked chickpeas; fava beans can also be used)
1 large tomato, chopped
1/2 teaspoon garlic powder
1-1/2 teaspoons chili powder

Sauté all the ingredients in a large frying pan over medium-high heat for 5 minutes. Add a little water, if necessary, to prevent sticking. Serve with rice or over a baked potato.

TOTAL CALORIES PER SERVING: 198   TOTAL FAT AS % OF DAILY VALUE: 3%
PROTEIN: 8 gm   CARBOHYDRATES: 38 gm   FAT: 2 gm
CALCIUM: 54 mg   IRON: 2 mg   SODIUM: 482 mg   DIETARY FIBER: 7 gm

SPICY POTATOES, CABBAGE, AND PEAS OVER RICE

(Serves 4)

2 Cups rice
4 Cups water
5 medium potatoes, peeled, and thinly sliced
2 Cups water
1/2 green cabbage
10-ounce box of frozen peas (or equivalent fresh)
2 teaspoons curry powder
1 teaspoon turmeric
1/2 teaspoon each ginger and garlic powder
1/8 teaspoon cayenne pepper
Salt to taste (optional)

Cook rice in 4 cups water in a covered pot over medium-high heat until done.

In a separate frying pan, add sliced potatoes to 2 cups of water and heat over medium-high heat. Shred cabbage and add to potatoes. Add peas and spices to mixture. Continue heating in covered pan, stirring occasionally, until potatoes are tender. Serve over cooked rice.

TOTAL CALORIES PER SERVING: 547   TOTAL FAT AS % OF DAILY VALUE: 2%
PROTEIN: 13 gm   CARBOHYDRATES: 121 gm   FAT: 1 gm
CALCIUM: 93 mg   IRON: 5 mg   SODIUM: 86 mg   DIETARY FIBER: 9 gm

CURRIED CHICKPEAS

(Serves 3)

Small onion, chopped
1 Tablespoon oil
19-ounce can chickpeas or garbanzo beans, drained
   (or 2 Cups cooked chickpeas)
1 Tablespoon curry powder
1/4 teaspoon black pepper

Sauté onion in oil over medium-high heat for 3 minutes. Add chickpeas and spices and continue heating for 3 more minutes, stirring occasionally. Serve hot with rice and/or steamed kale.

TOTAL CALORIES PER SERVING: 239   TOTAL FAT AS % OF DAILY VALUE: 9%
PROTEIN: 8 gm   CARBOHYDRATES: 38 gm   FAT: 6 gm
CALCIUM: 57 mg   IRON: 2 mg   SODIUM: 479 mg   DIETARY FIBER: 7 gm

VEGETABLE PANCAKES

(Serves 2)

2 Cups chopped vegetables (cabbage, carrots, celery, scallions, etc.)
1 Cup unbleached white flour
1 Cup water
1 Tablespoon soy sauce
1 teaspoon ginger powder (optional)
1 Tablespoon oil

Mix all the ingredients (except the oil) together in a large bowl.

Heat oil in non-stick frying pan over medium heat. Form six pancakes and fry on both sides until brown. After frying pancakes, lay them on a paper towel for a few minutes to drain off excess oil.

TOTAL CALORIES PER SERVING: 381   TOTAL FAT AS % OF DAILY VALUE: 11%
PROTEIN: 12 gm   CARBOHYDRATES: 68 gm   FAT: 7 gm
CALCIUM: 56 mg   IRON: 4 mg   SODIUM: 580 mg   DIETARY FIBER: 8 gm

CORN-STUFFED TOMATOES

(Serves 3)

6 large ripe tomatoes
1/4 Cup water
1 Cup frozen or fresh corn kernels
1/4 teaspoon cayenne pepper
1/2 Cup pitted black olives, chopped
1/2 Cup cornmeal
1/3 Cup water
2 Tablespoons molasses
1/2 teaspoon baking powder

Slice off tops of tomatoes and scoop out pulp and seeds.

Sauté corn, pepper, and olives in 1/4 cup water over medium heat for 3 minutes.

Mix cornmeal, 1/3 cup water, molasses, and baking powder together.

Fill tomatoes with corn mixture. Cover tops of tomatoes each with 1/6 of the cornmeal mixture.

Broil tomatoes for 10 minutes until the cornmeal topping becomes the texture of bread. Serve hot.

TOTAL CALORIES PER SERVING: 223   TOTAL FAT AS % OF DAILY VALUE: 6%
PROTEIN: 6 gm   CARBOHYDRATES: 47 gm   FAT: 4 gm
CALCIUM: 82 mg   IRON: 3 mg   SODIUM: 345 mg   DIETARY FIBER: 8 gm

BLACK-EYED PEAS AND COLLARDS

(Serves 4)

1-1/2 Tablespoons oil
2 cloves garlic, minced
10-ounce box frozen black-eyed peas
10-ounce box frozen collard greens
1/4 Cup water
2 Tablespoons lemon juice

Simmer oil, garlic, peas, and greens together in a covered frying pan over medium-high heat for 10 minutes, stirring occasionally. Add water and simmer for 10 more minutes. Add lemon juice. Heat 2 more minutes. Serve hot with rice.

TOTAL CALORIES PER SERVING: 149   TOTAL FAT AS % OF DAILY VALUE: 9%
PROTEIN: 7 gm   CARBOHYDRATES: 18 gm   FAT: 6 gm
CALCIUM: 79 mg   IRON: 3 mg   SODIUM: 50 mg   DIETARY FIBER: 6 gm

SPICY MILLET, CASHEWS, AND PEAS

(Serves 4)

1 Cup millet
3-1/2 Cups water
10-ounce box frozen peas
1/2 teaspoon each coriander, cumin, turmeric, and
   garlic powder
2 teaspoons soy sauce
2/3 Cup cashew pieces

Cook millet in water for 15 minutes over medium heat. Add remaining ingredients and continue cooking for 10 more minutes. Stir occasionally. Serve hot.

TOTAL CALORIES PER SERVING: 272   TOTAL FAT AS % OF DAILY VALUE: 18%
PROTEIN: 9 gm   CARBOHYDRATES: 35 gm   FAT: 12 gm
CALCIUM: 30 mg   IRON: 4 mg   SODIUM: 365 mg   DIETARY FIBER: unknown

KAREN'S BULGUR CHICK

(Serves 4)

1 medium onion, chopped
4 cloves garlic, minced
1 Tablespoon oil
Pepper to taste
1/2 Tablespoon parsley flakes
2-1/2 Cups water
1 Carrot, grated
1 Cup bulgur (cracked wheat)
19-ounce can chickpeas (garbanzo beans), drained (or
   2 Cups cooked chickpeas)

Sauté onion and garlic in oil until onion is transparent. Add the remaining ingredients to pot, except chickpeas. Simmer 15 minutes covered. Add chickpeas and simmer 10 minutes longer. Serve hot.

TOTAL CALORIES PER SERVING: 335   TOTAL FAT AS % OF DAILY VALUE: 8%
PROTEIN: 12 gm   CARBOHYDRATES: 61 gm   FAT: 5 gm
CALCIUM: 72 mg   IRON: 3 mg   SODIUM: 870 mg   DIETARY FIBER: 10 gm

FAVA BEAN DELIGHT

(Serves 3)

Small onion, chopped
1 Tablespoon oil
19-ounce can fava beans, drained
1 ripe tomato, chopped
Juice from 1/2 lemon
1 teaspoon cumin
1/8 teaspoon black pepper

Sauté onion in oil until transparent. Add remaining ingredients and cook over medium heat, stirring occasionally, for 10 more minutes. Serve hot with rice.

TOTAL CALORIES PER SERVING: 182   TOTAL FAT AS % OF DAILY VALUE: 8%
PROTEIN: 10 gm   CARBOHYDRATES: 26 gm   FAT: 5 gm
CALCIUM: 57 mg   IRON: 2 mg   SODIUM: 778 mg   DIETARY FIBER: 3 gm

BROCCOLI CHOW MEIN

(Serves 3)

3 stalks broccoli, chopped
1 Tablespoon oil
1/2 Cup water
1/2 pound mung bean sprouts

1/2 Cup slivered almonds or sunflower seeds (optional)
1 Tablespoon arrowroot starch or corn starch
1/2 Cup water
1-1/2 Tablespoons tamari or soy sauce
1 teaspoon sesame oil (optional)

Stir-fry broccoli in oil and 1/2 cup water for 3 minutes over medium-high heat. Add bean sprouts and almonds or seeds. Stir-fry for 2 more minutes.

Dissolve starch in 1/2 cup water. Add to broccoli and sprout mixture along with tamari or soy sauce and sesame oil if desired. Stir, then heat covered for 1 minute longer. Serve hot.

TOTAL CALORIES PER SERVING: 118   TOTAL FAT AS % OF DAILY VALUE: 8%
PROTEIN: 7 gm   CARBOHYDRATES: 16 gm   FAT: 5 gm
CALCIUM: 89 mg   IRON: 2 mg   SODIUM: 554 mg   DIETARY FIBER: 1 gm

BROCCOLI STIR-FRY

(Serves 4)

1 bunch broccoli, chopped
1 carrot, thinly sliced
2 stalks celery, chopped
1-1/2 Tablespoons sesame seeds
1 Tablespoon oil
1/2 Cup water

Stir-fry ingredients over medium-high heat for 8 minutes. Serve with rice; this dish is especially good with the lemony rice recipe found on page 54.

TOTAL CALORIES PER SERVING: 91   TOTAL FAT AS % OF DAILY VALUE: 8%
PROTEIN: 4 gm   CARBOHYDRATES: 9 gm   FAT: 5 gm
CALCIUM: 103 mg   IRON: 1 mg   SODIUM: 51 mg   DIETARY FIBER: 4 gm

SWEET SAUTÉED CABBAGE

(Serves 4)

2 Tablespoons vegan soy margarine
1 small cabbage, shredded
1/2 Cup raisins
2 teaspoons apple juice concentrate
1 teaspoon cinnamon
1 teaspoon caraway seeds

Sauté ingredients over medium heat for 10-15 minutes until cabbage is tender. Serve hot over rice.

TOTAL CALORIES PER SERVING: 142   TOTAL FAT AS % OF DAILY VALUE: 9%
PROTEIN: 2 gm   CARBOHYDRATES: 23 gm   FAT: 6 gm
CALCIUM: 62 mg   IRON: 1 mg   SODIUM: 87 mg   DIETARY FIBER: 6 gm

BOILED CABBAGE DISH

(Serves 4)

1/2 cabbage, shredded
2/3 Cup water
1 teaspoon oil
Small onion, chopped
1 tomato, chopped
1 teaspoon basil

Heat all the ingredients for 12-14 minutes over medium-high heat, until cabbage is tender. Serve hot over pasta or rice.

TOTAL CALORIES PER SERVING: 39   TOTAL FAT AS % OF DAILY VALUE: 2%
PROTEIN: 1 gm   CARBOHYDRATES: 7 gm   FAT: 1 gm
CALCIUM: 40 mg   IRON: 1 mg   SODIUM: 16 mg   DIETARY FIBER: 3 gm

SPICY RED LENTIL DISH

(Serves 3)

1 Tablespoon oil
1 Cup red lentils
1 onion, finely chopped
1 teaspoon cumin
1/4 teaspoon cayenne pepper
2-1/2 Cups water

Stir-fry lentils, onion, and spices in oil in non-stick frying pan for 2 minutes. Add water and cook over medium heat for 15 minutes in covered pot. Stir occasionally. Serve hot with rice.

Variation: Brown lentils may be used. However, they take longer to cook.

TOTAL CALORIES PER SERVING: 224   TOTAL FAT AS % OF DAILY VALUE: 9%
PROTEIN: 14 gm   CARBOHYDRATES: 32 gm   FAT: 6 gm
CALCIUM: 37 mg   IRON: 5 mg   SODIUM: 4 mg   DIETARY FIBER: 3 gm

FRIED EGGPLANT AND TOMATO STEW

(Serves 4)

1-1/2 pounds eggplant, peeled and sliced 1/4" thick
2 Tablespoons oil
15-ounce can tomato sauce
1 teaspoon oregano
1/2 teaspoon garlic powder

Fry eggplant on both sides in oil in a non-stick frying pan. (An electric frying pan is great for this dish.) Add water to prevent sticking.

Add sauce and spices. Heat for 5 minutes. Serve hot with rice or pasta.

TOTAL CALORIES PER SERVING: 178   % OF CALORIES FROM FAT: 11%
PROTEIN: 6 gm   CARBOHYDRATES: 28 gm   FAT: 7 gm
CALCIUM: 56 mg   IRON: 3 mg   SODIUM: 7 mg   DIETARY FIBER: unknown

CHINESE STIR-FRIED VEGETABLES AND PINEAPPLE

(Serves 4)

1 Tablespoon oil
1 Cup water
3 carrots, chopped
1 zucchini, chopped
6 ounces snowpeas (optional)
1/2 pound mushrooms, chopped
2 onions, sliced
2 large tomatoes, chopped
1/2 pound mung bean sprouts
10-ounce can crushed pineapple
3 Tablespoons soy sauce or tamari

Stir-fry all the ingredients together over medium-high heat until carrots are tender, yet crisp. Serve hot with rice.

Variation: Add baby corn and water chestnuts.

TOTAL CALORIES PER SERVING: 134   TOTAL FAT AS % OF DAILY VALUE: 3%
PROTEIN: 6 gm   CARBOHYDRATES: 27 gm   FAT: 2 gm
CALCIUM: 56 mg   IRON: 3 mg   SODIUM: 807 mg   DIETARY FIBER: 6 gm

BEAN TACOS

(Serves 6)

2 Tablespoons oil
1 large onion, chopped
2 cloves garlic, minced
19-ounce can kidney beans (or 2 cups cooked kidney
    beans), drained and mashed
1 Cup frozen or fresh corn kernels
1/4 teaspoon oregano
Salt and pepper to taste
Taco shells

Sauté onion and garlic in oil. Add mashed beans and corn. Add spices
and mix well. Heat 5-10 minutes over medium heat, stirring occasionally.
Add water if necessary to prevent sticking. Serve in heated taco shells
with shredded lettuce and chopped tomatoes.

TOTAL CALORIES PER SERVING: 198   TOTAL FAT AS % OF DAILY VALUE: 11%
PROTEIN: 7 gm   CARBOHYDRATES: 28 gm   FAT: 7 gm
CALCIUM: 46 mg   IRON: 2 mg   SODIUM: 380 mg   DIETARY FIBER: 6 gm

PUMPKIN CASSEROLE

(Serves 5)

29-ounce can unsweetened pumpkin
3 apples, chopped
1 Cup raisins
2 teaspoons cinnamon
1/4 teaspoon nutmeg
2 Tablespoons molasses
1/2 Cup chopped walnuts

Preheat oven to 375 degrees.

Mix all the ingredients together and pour into a loaf pan. Bake at 375 degrees for 20 minutes. Serve hot.

TOTAL CALORIES PER SERVING: 297   % OF CALORIES FROM FAT: 12%
PROTEIN: 6 gm   CARBOHYDRATES: 58 gm   FAT: 8 gm
CALCIUM: 94 mg   IRON: 4 mg   SODIUM: 15 mg   DIETARY FIBER: 8 gm

RUTH'S TASTY SEITAN

(Serves 2)

8-ounce package seitan, thinly sliced
1-1/2 Tablespoons oil
1/2 teaspoon garlic powder
1/2 teaspoon onion powder
1/4 teaspoon paprika
1/4 teaspoon salt
Pepper to taste
1 Tablespoon whole wheat flour
1 Cup water

Heat seitan, oil, and spices over medium-high heat for 5 minutes, stirring occasionally. Add flour and water and heat for 2 minutes longer. Serve hot over mashed potatoes, rice, or pasta.

Variation: Substitute wheat gluten for seitan.

TOTAL CALORIES PER SERVING: 239   TOTAL FAT AS % OF DAILY VALUE: 15%
PROTEIN: 21 gm   CARBOHYDRATES: 16 gm   FAT: 10 gm
CALCIUM: 23 mg   IRON: 4 mg   SODIUM: 277 mg   DIETARY FIBER: unknown

SEITAN SAUTÉ

(Serves 2)

1/2 Cup vegetable broth
Small onion, minced
1 apple, diced
1/2 Cup raisins
8-ounce package seitan, cubed

Sauté ingredients over medium heat for 5 minutes. Serve hot.

Variation: Substitute wheat gluten for seitan.

TOTAL CALORIES PER SERVING: 313   TOTAL FAT AS % OF DAILY VALUE: <1%
PROTEIN: 23 gm   CARBOHYDRATES: 59 gm   FAT: <1 gm
CALCIUM: 55 mg   IRON: 5 mg   SODIUM: 8 mg   DIETARY FIBER: unknown

BREADED SEITAN

(Serves 3)

8-ounce package seitan, sliced
1/3 Cup nutritional yeast
1 teaspoon garlic powder
1/2 teaspoon each cumin and coriander
1/8 teaspoon pepper
2 Tablespoons soy sauce or tamari
2 Tablespoons oil

Combine the yeast and spices in a small bowl. Dip seitan in soy sauce or tamari, then in yeast/spice mixture. Fry in oil on both sides until brown over medium-high heat.

Variation: Substitute wheat gluten for seitan.

TOTAL CALORIES PER SERVING: 214   TOTAL FAT AS % OF DAILY VALUE: 14%
PROTEIN: 20 gm   CARBOHYDRATES: 15 gm   FAT: 9 gm
CALCIUM: 45 mg   IRON: 5 mg   SODIUM: 362 mg   DIETARY FIBER: unknown

PASTA DISHES

CREAMED BROCCOLI AND PASTA

(Serves 5)

1 pound pasta
4 stalks broccoli, chopped
2 Cups soy milk
1/2 Cup nutritional yeast
1/2 teaspoon basil
1/2 teaspoon onion powder
1/4 teaspoon black pepper
1 Tablespoon vegan soy margarine
Salt to taste (optional)

Cook pasta in water. Steam chopped broccoli in separate pot.

Mix soy milk, yeast, spices, and margarine together in a small pot. Heat over medium heat until mixture begins to bubble.

Drain pasta and mix with broccoli. Pour heated sauce over pasta and broccoli. Serve.

TOTAL CALORIES PER SERVING: 398   TOTAL FAT AS % OF DAILY VALUE: 9%
PROTEIN: 20 gm   CARBOHYDRATES: 68 gm   FAT: 6 gm
CALCIUM: 140 mg   IRON: 6 mg   SODIUM: 123 mg   DIETARY FIBER: 10 gm

HEARTY MACARONI DINNER

(Serves 4)

2 Cups elbow macaroni
4 Cups water
1 onion, chopped
2 Tablespoons oil
3 Cups no salt added tomato juice
4 teaspoons chili powder
Salt and pepper to taste
10-ounce box frozen corn
19-ounce can kidney beans, drained (or 2 Cups cooked
    kidney beans)

Cook pasta in water until tender. Drain.

Sauté onion in oil in a large pot. Add remaining ingredients, as well as
cooked pasta. Simmer 15 minutes, stirring occasionally. Serve hot.

TOTAL CALORIES PER SERVING: 449   TOTAL FAT AS % OF DAILY VALUE: 14%
PROTEIN: 16 gm   CARBOHYDRATES: 82 gm   FAT: 9 gm
CALCIUM: 66 mg   IRON: 4 mg   SODIUM: 646 mg   DIETARY FIBER: 11 gm

BAKED BEAN AND PASTA CASSEROLE

(Serves 6)

19-ounce can pinto or kidney beans, drained (or 2 Cups
    cooked pinto or kidney beans)
3 Tablespoons molasses
Small onion, finely minced
4 Cups cooked pasta, drained
Dash of salt (optional)

Preheat oven to 350 degrees. Mix all the ingredients together. Pour into casserole dish and bake at 350 degrees for 15-20 minutes. Serve hot.

TOTAL CALORIES PER SERVING: 203   TOTAL FAT AS % OF DAILY VALUE: 2%
PROTEIN: 8 gm   CARBOHYDRATES: 42 gm   FAT: 1 gm
CALCIUM: 60 mg   IRON: 3 mg   SODIUM: 295 mg   DIETARY FIBER: 6 gm

BROCCOLI PASTA DISH

(Serves 4)

2 Tablespoons oil
3 scallions, chopped
1-2 stalks of broccoli, chopped
1 Cup shredded cabbage
8 ounces elbow macaroni, cooked and drained
15-ounce can black-eyed peas, drained
1 teaspoon sesame oil
Black bean sauce (optional)

Heat oil in a wok or large frying pan. Add scallions and broccoli. Sauté until broccoli is tender, but crisp. Add cabbage, cooked pasta, and peas. Stir-fry five minutes. Add sesame oil and black bean sauce to taste. Stir for a few more minutes over heat. Serve hot.

Note: Black bean sauce can be found in Asian grocery stores.

TOTAL CALORIES PER SERVING: 298   TOTAL FAT AS % OF DAILY VALUE: 14%
PROTEIN: 10 gm   CARBOHYDRATES: 46 gm   FAT: 9 gm
CALCIUM: 60 mg   IRON: 3 mg   SODIUM: 35 mg   DIETARY FIBER: 6 gm

CHICKPEA SAUCE

(Serves 4)

19-ounce can chickpeas or garbanzo beans, drained (or
**   2 Cups cooked chickpeas)**
15-ounce can tomato sauce
6-ounce can tomato paste
1 teaspoon onion powder
1 Tablespoon basil
Pinch of black pepper and salt

Simmer ingredients for 5 minutes over low heat, stirring occasionally.
When hot, pour over cooked spinach pasta or other type of pasta.

TOTAL CALORIES PER SERVING: 190   TOTAL FAT AS % OF DAILY VALUE: 3%
PROTEIN: 8 gm   CARBOHYDRATES: 38 gm   FAT: 2 gm
CALCIUM: 60 mg   IRON: 3 mg   SODIUM: 1037 mg   DIETARY FIBER: 5 gm

CHICKPEA BALLS FOR PASTA

(Serves 3)

19-ounce can chickpeas or garbanzo beans, drained (or
**   2 cups cooked chickpeas), mashed**
1/4 Cup whole wheat flour
1/8 teaspoon black pepper
1/4 teaspoon onion powder
1 stalk celery, finely chopped
2 Tablespoons oil

Mix all the ingredients together in a bowl. Form 1-1/2" balls and fry in oil
over a medium heat until brown on all sides. Serve with spaghetti and
your favorite tomato sauce.

Variation: Serve chickpea balls by themselves as a side dish.

TOTAL CALORIES PER SERVING: 312   TOTAL FAT AS % OF DAILY VALUE: 17%
PROTEIN: 9 gm   CARBOHYDRATES: 44 gm   FAT: 11 gm
CALCIUM: 60 mg   IRON: 3 mg   SODIUM: 491 mg   DIETARY FIBER: 7 gm

PASTA WITH SPICY TAHINI SAUCE

(Serves 5)

1 Tablespoon toasted sesame oil
1/2 Cup tahini (sesame butter)
2 Tablespoons lemon juice
1-1/2 teaspoons diced hot cherry peppers
1 teaspoon garlic powder
1 pound of pasta, cooked and drained

Mix together all ingredients (except cooked pasta). Pour sauce over cooked pasta, toss, and serve.

TOTAL CALORIES PER SERVING: 366   TOTAL FAT AS % OF DAILY VALUE: 17%
PROTEIN: 10 gm   CARBOHYDRATES: 58 gm   FAT: 11 gm
CALCIUM: 193 mg   IRON: 4 mg   SODIUM: 48 mg   DIETARY FIBER: 3 gm

BARBARA'S KALE CREAM SAUCE OVER PASTA

(Serves 5)

1 pound pasta, cooked and drained
1 Tablespoon vegan soy margarine
2 Tablespoons whole wheat flour
1 Cup soy milk
3 Tablespoons nutritional yeast
1/2 to 1 teaspoon each basil, thyme, dill, garlic powder
Salt and pepper to taste
10-ounce box frozen kale

Heat all ingredients (except pasta) together in pan over medium heat, stirring often, until kale is done. Pour sauce over cooked pasta and serve.

TOTAL CALORIES PER SERVING: 339   TOTAL FAT AS % OF DAILY VALUE: 8%
PROTEIN: 13 gm   CARBOHYDRATES: 62 gm   FAT: 5 gm
CALCIUM: 86 mg   IRON: 4 mg   SODIUM: 58 mg   DIETARY FIBER: 4 gm

SOY PRODUCTS

Please note: Tofu has become a common food in the United States. Most supermarkets now sell tofu. On the other hand, tempeh is somewhat difficult to find in American shops. The best place to buy tempeh is in a natural foods store. Since tempeh can be stored in your freezer, you may want to purchase several packages once you have located some.

TEMPEH STROGANOFF

(Serves 4)

10-ounce package tempeh, cubed
1 carrot, thinly chopped
2 stalks celery, chopped
1 small onion, minced
1 Tablespoon oil
1/2 teaspoon each basil, coriander, cumin, and garlic
    powder
1/8 teaspoon nutmeg
Salt to taste
2 Cups lowfat soy milk
2 Tablespoons nutritional yeast
2 Tablespoons whole wheat flour

Sauté cubed tempeh, carrot, celery, onion, and spices in oil over medium-high heat until tempeh is lightly browned. Stir often while sautéing. Lower heat to medium and add soy milk, yeast, and flour. Stir until a thick sauce forms and turn off heat. Serve hot over brown rice or pasta.

TOTAL CALORIES PER SERVING: 253   TOTAL FAT AS % OF DAILY VALUE: 15%
PROTEIN: 18 gm   CARBOHYDRATES: 28 gm   FAT: 10 gm
CALCIUM: 134 mg   IRON: 3 mg   SODIUM: 56 mg   DIETARY FIBER: 2 gm

SWEET TEMPEH CABBAGE SAUTÉ

(Serves 4)

1/2 Cup vegetable broth
10-ounce package tempeh, cubed
8 cabbage leaves, shredded
1 small onion, minced
3 ripe peaches, chopped

Sauté all the ingredients over medium-high heat for 8 minutes. Serve hot.

TOTAL CALORIES PER SERVING: 179   TOTAL FAT AS % OF DAILY VALUE: 8%
PROTEIN: 14 gm   CARBOHYDRATES: 22 gm   FAT: 5 gm
CALCIUM: 82 mg   IRON: 2 mg   SODIUM: 8 mg   DIETARY FIBER: 3 gm

TEMPEH BROCCOLI SAUTÉ

(Serves 4)

10-ounce package tempeh, cubed
2 stalks broccoli, chopped
1 small onion, minced
2 Tablespoons oil
2 teaspoons tamari or soy sauce (optional)

Sauté cubed tempeh, broccoli, and onion in oil over medium-high heat until tempeh is lightly browned. Add soy sauce at last moment. Serve with brown rice.

TOTAL CALORIES PER SERVING: 227   TOTAL FAT AS % OF DAILY VALUE: 18%
PROTEIN: 16 gm   CARBOHYDRATES: 18 gm   FAT: 12 gm
CALCIUM: 109 mg   IRON: 2 mg   SODIUM: 22 mg   DIETARY FIBER: 1 gm

TEMPEH/RICE POCKET SANDWICHES

(Makes 6 small pita sandwiches)

10-ounce package tempeh, cubed
1 onion, chopped
1 Tablespoon oil
1-1/2 Cups basmati rice
3-1/4 Cups water
1/2 Cup nutritional yeast
1/3 Cup whole wheat flour
1 Tablespoon garlic powder
1/4 Cup oil
1-2/3 Cups water
2 Tablespoons tamari or soy sauce
Pepper to taste
6 small pita bread pockets

Sauté cubed tempeh and onion in 1 Tablespoon oil over medium-high heat until tempeh is lightly browned. Meanwhile, cook rice in 3-1/4 cups water in a separate pot until done.

To make a gravy, mix the yeast, flour, garlic powder, 1/4 cup oil, 1-2/3 cups water, tamari or soy sauce, and pepper together in a frying pan. Stir over medium heat for a few minutes until gravy thickens and is hot.

Mix the tempeh mixture and cooked rice together. Stuff into pita bread pockets. Pour gravy over tempeh/rice mixture and serve right away.

TOTAL CALORIES PER SERVING: 342   TOTAL FAT AS % OF DAILY VALUE: 9%
PROTEIN: 18 gm   CARBOHYDRATES: 56 gm   FAT: 6 gm
CALCIUM: 90 mg   IRON: 5 mg   SODIUM: 364 mg   DIETARY FIBER: 1 gm

BARBECUED TEMPEH AND PEACHES

(Serves 4)

10-ounce package tempeh, cubed
2 Tablespoons oil
4 small ripe peaches, chopped
1 small onion, minced
8-ounce can no salt added tomato sauce
1/3 Cup each vinegar and reduced sodium soy sauce
1/4 teaspoon cayenne
1/2 teaspoon ginger
1 Tablespoon molasses

Preheat oven to 400 degrees. Sauté cubed tempeh in oil over medium-high heat for 2 minutes. Add chopped peaches and onion. Sauté 5 minutes longer. Mix tomato sauce, vinegar, soy sauce, spices, and molasses together. Pour tempeh/peach mixture into a casserole dish. Cover with sauce and bake for 20 minutes at 400 degrees. Serve hot.

Variation: Substitute 6 fresh apricots for the peaches and/or substitute 1 pound of tofu for tempeh.

TOTAL CALORIES PER SERVING: 288   TOTAL FAT AS % OF DAILY VALUE: 18%
PROTEIN: 16 gm   CARBOHYDRATES: 34 gm   FAT: 12 gm
CALCIUM: 102 mg   IRON: 3 mg   SODIUM: 904 mg   DIETARY FIBER: 4 gm

CURRIED TEMPEH AND RICE DISH

(Serves 3-4)

1 Cup basmati rice
2-1/2 Cups water
1 onion, chopped
1 Tablespoon oil
10-ounce package tempeh, cubed

1/4 cup water
1 Cup frozen or fresh peas
1 teaspoon tamari or soy sauce
2 teaspoons curry powder
1/2 teaspoon garlic powder
1/4 teaspoon black pepper

Cook rice in water until done. In a separate frying pan, sauté onion in oil for 2 minutes. Add cubed tempeh, water, peas, tamari or soy sauce, and spices. Stir-fry for 8 minutes. Serve over cooked rice.

TOTAL CALORIES PER SERVING: 504   TOTAL FAT AS % OF DAILY VALUE: 18%
PROTEIN: 25 gm   CARBOHYDRATES: 76 gm   FAT: 12 gm
CALCIUM: 129 mg   IRON: 5 mg   SODIUM: 173 mg   DIETARY FIBER: 4 gm

SCRAMBLED TOFU AND BOK CHOY

(Serves 4)

1-1/2 teaspoons oil
1/2 pound bok choy, chopped (stems and leaves)
12 snowpeas
Shake of black pepper
1 small onion, minced
1 teaspoon turmeric (optional)
1 pound tofu, crumbled
1 Tablespoon tamari or soy sauce

Sauté all the ingredients except the tofu and tamari or soy sauce for 2 minutes over medium-high heat. Add the tofu and tamari or soy sauce and sauté 2 minutes longer. Serve hot for breakfast or lunch.

TOTAL CALORIES PER SERVING: 124   TOTAL FAT AS % OF DAILY VALUE: 11%
PROTEIN: 11 gm   CARBOHYDRATES: 6 gm   FAT: 7 gm
CALCIUM: 190 mg   IRON: 7 mg   SODIUM: 303 mg   DIETARY FIBER: unknown

TOFU/SQUASH SCRAMBLE

(Serves 2)

1/4 Cup vegetable broth
1 medium yellow squash or zucchini, finely chopped
1/2 small onion, minced
1/4 teaspoon pepper
2 teaspoons basil
1/2 pound tofu, crumbled
1/4 teaspoon tamari or soy sauce (optional)

Sauté all the ingredients except the tofu and tamari or soy sauce
together over medium-high heat until the squash begins to soften.
Add tofu and tamari or soy sauce and continue sautéing for another
3-5 minutes. Serve hot.

TOTAL CALORIES PER SERVING: 119   TOTAL FAT AS % OF DAILY VALUE: 9%
PROTEIN: 11 gm   CARBOHYDRATES: 9 gm   FAT: 6 gm
CALCIUM: 151 mg   IRON: 7 mg   SODIUM: 11 mg   DIETARY FIBER: 3 gm

TOFU-STUFFED SNOWPEA PODS

(Serves 4-5)

1/4 pound snowpeas (about 30)
1/2 pound tofu, crumbled
1 teaspoon vinegar
2 Tablespoons water
1/2 teaspoon caraway seeds

Pinch off ends of snow pea pods. Slit pods open length-wise. Blend tofu
with vinegar, water, and caraway seeds in a food processor until creamy.
Stuff pods with tofu mixture and serve chilled.

TOTAL CALORIES PER SERVING: 58   TOTAL FAT AS % OF DAILY VALUE: 5%
PROTEIN: 6 gm   CARBOHYDRATES: 4 gm   FAT: 3 gm
CALCIUM: 72 mg   IRON: 3 mg   SODIUM: 4 mg   DIETARY FIBER: unknown

TOFU-STUFFED CHERRY TOMATOES

(Serves 4)

1/2 pound cherry tomatoes
1/2 pound tofu, crumbled
1/2 teaspoon oregano
1/4 teaspoon garlic powder
1/4 teaspoon turmeric (optional)
Salt and pepper to taste

Remove stems from cherry tomatoes and carefully cut a small hole in the top of each tomato. Remove and save tomato pulp.

In a small bowl mix tofu, tomato pulp, and spices. Stuff cherry tomatoes with this mixture and serve chilled.

TOTAL CALORIES PER SERVING: 55   TOTAL FAT AS % OF DAILY VALUE: 5%
PROTEIN: 5 gm   CARBOHYDRATES: 4 gm   FAT: 3 gm
CALCIUM: 65 mg   IRON: 3 mg   SODIUM: 8 mg   DIETARY FIBER: 2 gm

TOFU DILL DIP

(Serves 5)

1 cucumber, peeled
1 pound tofu, crumbled

1 teaspoon dill weed
2 Tablespoons lemon juice
1/4 Cup fresh parsley, chopped or 1 Tablespoon dried
    parsley
1/2 teaspoon garlic powder
Salt to taste

Place all the ingredients into a food processor or blender and blend until creamy. Serve with raw vegetables or crackers.

TOTAL CALORIES PER SERVING: 77   TOTAL FAT AS % OF DAILY VALUE: 8%
PROTEIN: 8 gm   CARBOHYDRATES: 3 gm   FAT: 5 gm
CALCIUM: 104 mg   IRON: 5 mg   SODIUM: 8 mg   DIETARY FIBER: 1 gm

TOFU DIP

(Serves 5)

1 pound tofu, crumbled
1/4 Cup vegan eggless mayonnaise
1/2 teaspoon garlic or onion powder
1 Tablespoon tamari or soy sauce
1/4 Cup nutritional yeast
1/4 Cup water

Place all the ingredients together in a food processor or blender and blend until creamy. Serve with raw vegetables or crackers.

TOTAL CALORIES PER SERVING: 123   TOTAL FAT AS % OF DAILY VALUE: 12%
PROTEIN: 11 gm   CARBOHYDRATES: 5 gm   FAT: 8 gm
CALCIUM: 112 mg   IRON: 6 mg   SODIUM: 256 mg   DIETARY FIBER: 1 gm

TOFU SPREAD

(Serves 7)

1 pound tofu, crumbled
1 small onion, chopped
1 carrot, grated
2 stalks celery, chopped
1/4 Cup tahini (sesame butter)
2 teaspoons lemon juice
Salt to taste (optional)

Place ingredients into a food processor or blender and blend for 2-3 minutes. Serve spread on whole wheat bread with lettuce or sprouts.

TOTAL CALORIES PER SERVING: 94   TOTAL FAT AS % OF DAILY VALUE: 9%
PROTEIN: 7 gm   CARBOHYDRATES: 6 gm   FAT: 6 gm
CALCIUM: 142 mg   IRON: 4 mg   SODIUM: 35 mg   DIETARY FIBER: 2 gm

AVOCADO TOFU SPREAD

(Serves 4)

1 ripe avocado, peeled
1 ripe tomato
1/2 pound tofu, crumbled
1/4 teaspoon cayenne pepper
1/2 teaspoon each onion powder and garlic powder

Place all the ingredients in a food processor or blender and blend until creamy. Serve with raw vegetables or crackers.

TOTAL CALORIES PER SERVING: 131   TOTAL FAT AS % OF DAILY VALUE: 17%
PROTEIN: 6 gm   CARBOHYDRATES: 6 gm   FAT: 11 gm
CALCIUM: 69 mg   IRON: 4 mg   SODIUM: 12 mg   DIETARY FIBER: unknown

TOFU MUSHROOM SAUCE

(Serves 5)

1 pound tofu, cubed or crumbled
1/2 pound small mushrooms
1 teaspoon garlic powder
1 teaspoon basil
1 Tablespoon oil
15-ounce can tomato sauce

Sauté tofu and mushrooms with spices in oil for 5 minutes. Add sauce and continue heating 5 minutes longer. Serve hot over your favorite cooked pasta.

TOTAL CALORIES PER SERVING: 134   TOTAL FAT AS % OF DAILY VALUE: 12%
PROTEIN: 10 gm   CARBOHYDRATES: 11 gm   FAT: 8 gm
CALCIUM: 113 mg IRON: 6 mg SODIUM: 572 mg DIETARY FIBER: 8 gm

SPICY TOFU SAUTÉ

(Serves 4)

1/4 Cup water
1 Cup frozen or fresh corn kernels
1/2 Cup raisins
1 pound tofu, crumbled
1 teaspoon sesame seeds (optional)
1 Tablespoon tamari or soy sauce
1/4 teaspoon cayenne pepper

Sauté all ingredients for 5 minutes over medium-high heat. Lower heat and cover pan. Allow to simmer a few minutes longer. Remove from heat and serve hot.

Variation: Stir in 1 Tablespoon sesame oil right before serving.

TOTAL CALORIES PER SERVING: 185   TOTAL FAT AS % OF DAILY VALUE: 9%
PROTEIN: 11 gm   CARBOHYDRATES: 27 gm   FAT: 6 gm
CALCIUM: 135 mg   IRON: 7 mg   SODIUM: 400 mg   DIETARY FIBER: 4 gm

TOFU "CODDIES"

(Serves 4)

1/2 pound tofu, crumbled
1 Cup water
2 potatoes, canned or boiled and peeled
1/2 Cup whole wheat pastry flour
1 Tablespoon tamari or soy sauce
2 Tablespoons Old Bay Seasoning
1 Cup wheat germ
2 teaspoons oil

Blend tofu, water, and potatoes in a food processor. Add flour, tamari or soy sauce, and seasoning to blended mixture to form a stiff dough. Roll into patties and dredge in wheat germ. Fry in lightly oiled pan until golden brown on each side. Drain on paper towels before serving.

TOTAL CALORIES PER SERVING: 234   TOTAL FAT AS % OF DAILY VALUE: 11%
PROTEIN: 13 gm   CARBOHYDRATES: 34 gm   FAT: 7 gm
CALCIUM: 85 mg   IRON: 6 mg   SODIUM: 265 mg   DIETARY FIBER: 7 gm

TOFU SQUASH BURGERS

(Serves 3)

1/2 pound tofu, crumbled
1 pound yellow squash, grated
1/2 Cup each whole wheat flour and toasted wheat
    germ
1 small onion, minced

1 teaspoon tarragon
1 Tablespoon tamari or soy sauce
1/4 teaspoon pepper
1 Tablespoon oil

Mix all the ingredients (except oil) in a bowl. Form 6 patties and fry in oil over medium-high heat for 5 minutes until brown on one side. Turn and fry 5 minutes longer. Serve hot on whole wheat buns.

TOTAL CALORIES PER SERVING: 247   TOTAL FAT AS % OF DAILY VALUE: 15%
PROTEIN: 14 gm   CARBOHYDRATES: 30 gm   FAT: 10 gm
CALCIUM: 135 mg   IRON: 7 mg   SODIUM: 353 mg   DIETARY FIBER: 8 gm

BROCCOLI AND TOFU SAUTÉ

(Serves 4)

1/2 Cup vegetable broth
1 bunch broccoli, chopped (stems included)
1 inch ginger root, grated
2 cloves garlic, minced
3 scallions, chopped
1 Tablespoon vinegar
2 Tablespoons tamari or soy sauce
1 pound tofu, crumbled

Sauté all the ingredients, except tofu, until broccoli is tender. Add tofu and stir-fry 5 minutes longer. Serve with brown rice.

TOTAL CALORIES PER SERVING: 130   TOTAL FAT AS % OF DAILY VALUE: 8%
PROTEIN: 14 gm   CARBOHYDRATES: 11 gm   FAT: 5 gm
CALCIUM: 194 mg   IRON: 7 mg   SODIUM: 551 mg   DIETARY FIBER: 5 gm

SPICY SAUTÉED TOFU WITH PEAS

(Serves 4)

2 pounds tofu, cut into small cubes
1 Tablespoon oil
1/4 Cup water
1 teaspoon dill weed
1/2 teaspoon each basil, cumin, turmeric, and curry
2 cloves garlic, minced
2 Tablespoons tamari or soy sauce
1/4 Cup nutritional yeast (optional)
10-ounce box frozen peas, thawed
1/2 Cup cashew pieces (optional)

Stir-fry all the ingredients except the peas and cashews for 5 minutes over medium-high heat. Add peas and cashews and heat 5 minutes longer over low heat. Serve hot.

TOTAL CALORIES PER SERVING: 256   TOTAL FAT AS % OF DAILY VALUE: 23%
PROTEIN: 22 gm   CARBOHYDRATES: 14 gm   FAT: 15 gm
CALCIUM: 261 mg   IRON: 14 mg   SODIUM: 580 mg   DIETARY FIBER: 6 gm

TOFU STEW

(Serves 4)

1 pound tofu, cubed in small pieces
1-1/2 teaspoons oil
1 small zucchini, chopped
1 carrot, peeled and sliced thinly
2 stalks celery, chopped finely
1 pound mushrooms, sliced
1/2 teaspoon garlic powder
Pinch black pepper

1/2 teaspoon oregano
1 small onion
3 Tablespoons vegetable broth
3 Tablespoons whole wheat flour
1 Tablespoon tamari or soy sauce
1/4 teaspoon paprika
1 Cup water

Sauté tofu, zucchini, carrot, celery, mushrooms, and spices in oil in non-stick pan for 10 minutes over medium-high heat. Lower heat and simmer 5 minutes longer in a covered pan.

While tofu and vegetables are simmering, stir-fry onion in broth until clear. Add flour, tamari or soy sauce, paprika, and water. Stir until sauce begins to thicken. Add tofu and vegetable mixture to sauce. Stir well and serve hot.

TOTAL CALORIES PER SERVING: 219   TOTAL FAT AS % OF DAILY VALUE: 18%
PROTEIN: 14 gm   CARBOHYDRATES: 18 gm   FAT: 12 gm
CALCIUM: 153 mg   IRON: 8 mg   SODIUM: 295 mg   DIETARY FIBER: 6 gm

TOFU CASSEROLE

(Serves 6)

2 Tablespoons oil
1 onion, chopped
1/2 pound mushrooms, chopped
1/2 pound zucchini, chopped
1 carrot, chopped
Two 10-ounce boxes frozen spinach
1 teaspoon salt (optional)
1 teaspoon garlic powder
1-1/2 pounds tofu, crumbled
1/2 Cup nutritional yeast

Sauté onion, mushrooms, zucchini, and carrot in oil over medium-high heat for 5 minutes. Add spinach and spices. Heat 10 minutes, stirring occasionally. Mix vegetables with crumbled tofu and yeast and continue heating for 5 minutes. Press into a casserole dish and serve warm.

TOTAL CALORIES PER SERVING: 199   TOTAL FAT AS % OF DAILY VALUE: 15%
PROTEIN: 17 gm   CARBOHYDRATES: 17 gm   FAT: 10 gm
CALCIUM: 279 mg   IRON: 9 mg   SODIUM: 108 mg   DIETARY FIBER: 6 gm

TOFU ITALIANO

(Serves 4)

1 pound pasta
1 onion, chopped
2 Tablespoons oil
1 pound tofu, cubed
10-ounce box each frozen corn and frozen peas
1/2 teaspoon each oregano and garlic powder
15-ounce can tomato sauce

Pre-cook pasta in water according to directions. Sauté onion and tofu in oil over medium-high heat for 5 minutes. Add remaining ingredients and cook 10 minutes longer, stirring occasionally. Serve over cooked pasta.

TOTAL CALORIES PER SERVING: 309   TOTAL FAT AS % OF DAILY VALUE: 22%
PROTEIN: 16 gm   CARBOHYDRATES: 38 gm   FAT: 14 gm
CALCIUM: 159 mg   IRON: 9 mg   SODIUM: 773 mg   DIETARY FIBER: 8 gm

KAREN'S SLOPPY TOFU

(Serves 3)

1 small onion, chopped
4 cloves garlic, minced
1 Tablespoon oil
Pepper to taste

3 large mushrooms, chopped
1 carrot, grated (optional)
1/2 Tablespoon dried parsley
1/2 pound tofu, crumbled
2 teaspoons tamari or soy sauce (optional)
3 Tablespoons tomato sauce

Sauté onion and garlic in oil until onion is clear. Add pepper, mushrooms, carrot, and parsley. Add tofu, tamari or soy sauce, and sauce. Cook, stirring occasionally, until heated through. Serve as a sandwich filling, sprinkled with nutritional yeast.

TOTAL CALORIES PER SERVING: 124   TOTAL FAT AS % OF DAILY VALUE: 12%
PROTEIN: 8 gm   CARBOHYDRATES: 6 gm   FAT: 8 gm
CALCIUM: 98 mg   IRON: 5 mg   SODIUM: 107 mg   DIETARY FIBER: 1 gm

WAYNE'S TOFU CHILI

(Serves 8)

1 pound tofu, cubed in small pieces
2 Tablespoons oil
2 onions, chopped
3 green peppers, chopped
28-ounce can crushed tomatoes
15-ounce can black-eyed peas, drained
15-ounce can kidney beans, drained
15-ounce can white beans, drained
2 jalapeño peppers, minced
Garlic and chili powder to taste

Sauté tofu in oil for 10 minutes. Add chopped onions and green peppers, and stir-fry 5 minutes longer. Lower heat. Add tomatoes, peas, beans, jalapeño peppers, and spices. Simmer for 12 minutes. You can add some tomato paste if sauce is too thin. You can also freeze the chili.

TOTAL CALORIES PER SERVING: 301   TOTAL FAT AS % OF DAILY VALUE: 11%
PROTEIN: 19 gm   CARBOHYDRATES: 43 gm   FAT: 7 gm
CALCIUM: 164 mg   IRON: 8 mg   SODIUM: 413 mg   DIETARY FIBER: 10 gm

DESSERTS

Please note: The best dessert for people on a low-fat diet is fresh fruit. If you are looking for a lowfat dessert in this section choose Baked Papaya, Creamy Rice Pudding, Ginger Cookies, or Chocolate Pudding. The remaining dessert recipes should be used on a limited basis.

HEAVENLY CHOCOLATE CUPCAKES

(Makes 18)

1 Cup molasses
1/2 Cup soy milk
2 Cups non-dairy, dark chocolate chips
6 Tablespoons vegan soy margarine
1 teaspoon vanilla extract
4 Tablespoons cornstarch
2 Cups unbleached white flour
1 teaspoon baking soda
1/2 Cup soy milk

Preheat oven to 375 degrees. Combine molasses, soy milk, and chips in a small pan. Heat on low, stirring occasionally, until chips melt. Remove from heat and add margarine, stirring until it softens. Add vanilla and cornstarch to mixture and stir. Add flour, baking soda, and soy milk. Mix ingredients well.

Lightly oil 18 muffin cups and divide the batter among them, filling each cup about half full. Bake 20 minutes at 375 degrees. Cool cupcakes before removing from tins.

Variations: Replace chocolate chips with non-dairy carob chips or add 3/4 cup chopped walnuts to batter before baking.

TOTAL CALORIES PER CUPCAKE: 231   TOTAL FAT AS % OF DAILY VALUE: 17%
PROTEIN: 3 gm   CARBOHYDRATES: 34 gm   FAT: 11 gm
CALCIUM: 65 mg   IRON: 2 mg   SODIUM: 119 mg   DIETARY FIBER: <1 gm

GINGER COOKIES

(Makes 2 dozen)

1/4 Cup vegan soy margarine
1/4 Cup molasses
1/3 cup water
1-1/2 Cups whole wheat pastry flour
1 teaspoon baking soda
1/2 teaspoon ginger powder
1/2 teaspoon cinnamon
1/4 teaspoon ground cloves

Preheat oven to 375 degrees. Mash soy margarine with a fork in a bowl. Add the remaining ingredients and stir well.

Form two dozen 1" round balls and place on a lightly oiled cookie sheet. Bake for 12 to 15 minutes at 375 degrees. Allow cookies to cool before removing from cookie sheet.

TOTAL CALORIES PER COOKIE: 49   TOTAL FAT AS % OF DAILY VALUE: 3%
PROTEIN: 1 gm   CARBOHYDRATES: 7 gm   FAT: 2 gm
CALCIUM: 13 mg   IRON: <1 mg   SODIUM: 70 mg   DIETARY FIBER: <1 gm

CAROB CHIP COOKIES

(Makes 2 dozen)

2/3 Cup water
2 Cups whole wheat flour
1 teaspoon baking soda
2 teaspoons vanilla extract
1/2 Cup oil or vegan soy margarine
1/2 Cup raisins
1/2 Cup peanuts
1/2 Cup non-dairy carob chips

Preheat oven to 375 degrees. Mix all the ingredients together in a large bowl. Spoon batter onto a lightly oiled cookie sheet, forming 24 cookies.

Bake 12-15 minutes at 375 degrees. Allow cookies to cool before removing from the cookie sheet.

TOTAL CALORIES PER COOKIE: 119   TOTAL FAT AS % OF DAILY VALUE: 12%
PROTEIN: 2 gm   CARBOHYDRATES: 12 gm   FAT: 8 gm
CALCIUM: 9 mg   IRON: 1 mg   SODIUM: 48 mg   DIETARY FIBER: 2 gm

FESTIVE CASHEW COOKIES

(Makes 2 dozen)

2 Cups raw cashews
1 Cup rolled oats
1 teaspoon cinnamon
1/3 Cup molasses or maple syrup
1/2 Cup water
1/4 Cup oil
1 teaspoon vanilla extract
Small jar fruit-only jam

Preheat oven to 375 degrees. Grind the raw cashews and rolled oats together in a food processor for a few minutes. Pour mixture into a large bowl and add the remaining ingredients, except the jam. Mix all the ingredients together.

Form 24 round balls and place on a lightly oiled cookie sheet. With your thumb, form a small well in the center of each ball. Place a small amount of jam in each well.

Bake for 15 minutes at 375 degrees. Allow cookies to cool before removing them from the cookie sheet. These cookies make a wonderful gift.

TOTAL CALORIES PER COOKIE: 125   TOTAL FAT AS % OF DAILY VALUE: 12%
PROTEIN: 2 gm   CARBOHYDRATES: 13 gm   FAT: 8 gm
CALCIUM: 20 mg   IRON: 1 mg   SODIUM: 71 mg   DIETARY FIBER: 1 gm

CAROB RAISIN PEANUT CLUSTERS

(Makes 2 dozen)

3 Cups non-dairy carob chips
1/2 Cup raisins
1/2 Cup shelled peanuts

Melt carob chips in a double boiler over medium heat. Add raisins and peanuts. Remove pot from stove and mix ingredients together.

Drop by spoonfuls onto a cookie sheet, forming two dozen clusters. Cool in refrigerator for at least 15 minutes and serve.

Variations: Substitute non-dairy dark chocolate chips for carob chips and/or substitute other dried fruit for the raisins and different nuts for the peanuts.

TOTAL CALORIES PER CLUSTER: 135   TOTAL FAT AS % OF DAILY VALUE: 14%
PROTEIN: 2 gm   CARBOHYDRATES: 15 gm   FAT: 9 gm
CALCIUM: 10 mg   IRON: 1 mg   SODIUM: 1 mg   DIETARY FIBER: 2 gm

CAKE-LIKE CHOCOLATE CHIP COOKIES

(Makes 2 dozen)

12-ounce package of non-dairy, dark chocolate chips
1 teaspoon baking soda
2-1/4 Cups whole wheat flour
1-1/2 teaspoons vanilla extract
1 large banana, mashed
1/4 Cup maple syrup
1/2 Cup water

Preheat oven to 375 degrees. Mix all the ingredients together in a bowl. Form 24 cookies on a lightly oiled cookie sheet.

Bake for 8-10 minutes at 375 degrees. Cool cookies before removing from the cookie sheet.

Variation: Add 1/2 cup chopped nuts to the batter before baking.

TOTAL CALORIES PER COOKIE: 122   TOTAL FAT AS % OF DAILY VALUE: 8%
PROTEIN: 2 gm   CARBOHYDRATES: 19 gm   FAT: 5 gm
CALCIUM: 10 mg   IRON: 1 mg   SODIUM: 48 mg   DIETARY FIBER: 1 gm

BAKED PEARS IN BLANKETS

(Serves 4)

2 ripe pears
1/2 teaspoon cinnamon
1/4 teaspoon nutmeg
3 Tablespoons vegan soy margarine
1-1/2 Cups unbleached white flour
1/2 Cup cold water
3 Tablespoons molasses
1 Tablespoon vegan soy margarine, melted

Preheat oven to 425 degrees. Slice each pear into 8 wedges and place them in a bowl. Sprinkle pears with cinnamon and nutmeg.

In a separate bowl, mash 3 Tablespoons soy margarine with a fork. Add the flour, cold water, and molasses. Mix ingredients well to form a soft dough. Roll dough out on a floured board. Cut into 16 long strips. Wrap each pear wedge with the dough and place it on a lightly oiled cookie sheet. Brush pear wedges with the melted margarine. Bake for 25 minutes at 425 degrees.

TOTAL CALORIES PER SERVING: 336   TOTAL FAT AS % OF DAILY VALUE: 17%
PROTEIN: 5 gm   CARBOHYDRATES: 55 gm   FAT: 11 gm
CALCIUM: 66 mg   IRON: 3 mg   SODIUM: 101 mg   DIETARY FIBER: 4 gm

10 VEGAN SUPERFOODS

These are examples of nutrient-rich vegan foods. Many other foods could be added to this list.

1. Lentils

2. Kale

3. Tofu

4. Fortified soymilk

5. Almonds

6. Sweet potatoes

7. Oranges

8. Broccoli

9. Quinoa

10. Chickpeas

Please note: If you are interested in receiving copies of the My Vegan Plate appearing on the next two pages email vrg@vrg.org with your street address or call (410) 366-8343 and let us know how many copies you would like.

Vegan
MY^PLATE

Nutrition Tips:

*Choose mostly whole grains.

*Eat a variety of foods from each of the food groups.

*Adults age 70 and younger need 600 IU of vitamin D daily.
Sources include fortified foods (such as some soymilks) or a vitamin D supplement.

*Sources of iodine include iodized salt (3/8 teaspoon daily) or
an iodine supplement (150 micrograms).

*See www.vrg.org for recipes and more details.

Calcium
leafy greens, calcium-fortified
soymilk and juices, tofu, etc.

Grains

Fruits

Text by Reed Mangels, PhD, RD
Design by Lindsey Siferd

Vitamin B12:

Vegans need a reliable source of vitamin B12. Eat daily a couple of servings of fortified foods such as B12-fortified soymilk, breakfast cereal, meat analog, or Vegetarian Support Formula nutritional yeast. Check the label for fortification. If fortified foods are not eaten daily, you should take a vitamin B12 supplement (25 micrograms daily).

Note:

Like any food plan, this should only serve as a general guide for adults. The plan can be modified according to your own personal needs. This is not personal medical advice. Individuals with special health needs should consult a registered dietitian or a medical doctor knowledgeable about vegan nutrition.

VRg. The Vegetarian Resource Group P.O. Box 1463 Baltimore, MD 21203 www.vrg.org (410) 366-8343

10 QUICK AND EASY VEGAN MEALS

1. Bean burritos (warmed tortillas filled with canned refried beans, chopped lettuce and tomato, salsa); corn on the cob; watermelon chunks

2. Quick-cooking pasta with jarred vegan sauce mixed with canned, drained chickpeas; French bread; tossed salad

3. Veggie burgers (commercial) on whole-wheat bun with the fixings; baked chips; carrot sticks

4. Stir-fried vegetables (use pre-cut veggies for convenience) with vegan "chicken" strips served over whole-wheat couscous

5. Hummus wraps with vegetables; fruit salad

6. Scrambled tofu with mushrooms and onions; whole-wheat toast; steamed broccoli

7. Mu shu vegetables – stir-fry shredded cabbage, carrots, and onions with soy sauce and spices; roll up in a flour tortilla with thin strips of baked tofu; top with vegan Hoisin sauce

8. Barbecued beans and potatoes – sauté drained canned black beans with pre-cooked cubed potatoes and vegan barbecue sauce; serve with sliced cucumber and cherry tomatoes

9. Peanut noodles – mix cooked pasta with a commercial vegan peanut-coconut sauce; add steamed vegetables and beans or tofu cubes

10. Chef salad – tossed salad from the supermarket salad bar topped with strips of vegan deli slices; toss with your favorite vegan dressing

BAKED PAPAYA

(Serves 4)

2 ripe papayas
4 Tablespoons frozen orange juice concentrate
1/2 teaspoon cinnamon

Preheat oven to 350 degrees. Remove skin from both papayas. Slice papayas and lay fruit in a baking dish. Sprinkle papaya with dabs of the frozen juice concentrate and cinnamon.

Bake for 20-25 minutes at 350 degrees. Serve hot.

TOTAL CALORIES PER SERVING: 88   TOTAL FAT AS % OF DAILY VALUE: <1%
PROTEIN: 1 gm   CARBOHYDRATES: 22 gm   FAT: <1 gm
CALCIUM: 42 mg   IRON: <1 mg   SODIUM: 5 mg   DIETARY FIBER: 1 gm

PUMPKIN PIE

(Makes 2 pies — Serves 12)

1-1/2 Cups soy milk
2 Tablespoons Ener-G Egg Replacer
16-ounce can puréed pumpkin (with no added sugar)
1/2 Cup maple syrup
1 teaspoon cinnamon
1/2 teaspoon ginger
2 vegan pie crusts

Preheat oven to 425 degrees. Blend the soy milk and Ener-G Egg Replacer together in a bowl using a whisk. Add the remaining ingredients and mix well.

Pour into two pre-made vegan pie crusts (available at some natural foods stores and supermarkets). Bake 20 minutes at 425 degrees. Remove pies from the oven and allow to cool before slicing and serving.

TOTAL CALORIES PER SERVING FILLING (NOT INCLUDING PIE SHELL): 221
TOTAL FAT AS % OF DAILY VALUE: 17%
PROTEIN: 4 gm   CARBOHYDRATES: 28 gm   FAT: 11 gm
CALCIUM: 47 mg   IRON: 2 mg   SODIUM: 202 mg   DIETARY FIBER: 1 gm

SOY WHIPPED CREAM

(Makes enough to top one pie)

1/4 Cup soy milk
1/2 Cup vegetable oil
1 Tablespoon maple syrup
1/2 teaspoon vanilla extract

Place soy milk and 1/4 cup oil in a blender. Blend at highest speed and slowly drizzle in remaining 1/4 cup oil. Blend in syrup and vanilla. Add a little more oil if necessary to thicken. Chill and serve.

Note: This recipe does not work well on damp, rainy days.

TOTAL CALORIES PER SERVING (1/6 recipe): 175   TOTAL FAT AS % OF DAILY
VALUE: 28%   PROTEIN: <1 gm   CARBOHYDRATES: 3 gm   FAT: 18 gm
CALCIUM: 4 mg   IRON: <1 mg   SODIUM: 5 mg   DIETARY FIBER: 0 gm

CHOCOLATE PUDDING

(Serves 3)

1-1/2 Cups soy milk
3 Tablespoons cornstarch
1/4 teaspoon vanilla
1/4 Cup maple syrup
1/4 Cup cocoa powder
2 bananas, sliced (optional)

Whisk all the ingredients (except the bananas) together in a pot. Cook over medium heat, stirring constantly until pudding thickens.

Remove pot from stove. Stir in sliced bananas if desired. Chill for at least 15 minutes before serving.

Variation: Replace chocolate powder with non-dairy carob powder.

TOTAL CALORIES PER SERVING: 198   TOTAL FAT AS % OF DAILY VALUE: 6%
PROTEIN: 7 gm   CARBOHYDRATES: 36 gm   FAT: 4 gm
CALCIUM: 92 mg   IRON: 1 mg   SODIUM: 155 mg   DIETARY FIBER: < 1 gm

KAREN'S CREAMY RICE PUDDING

(Serves 8)

2 Cups pre-cooked rice
1-1/2 teaspoons cinnamon
1 Tablespoon vanilla extract
1 Cup raisins
1/2 Cup slivered almonds (optional)
3-4 Cups soy milk

Mix all the ingredients together in a pot. Simmer until the mixture begins to thicken (15-20 minutes), stirring occasionally.

Remove from stove and serve hot or cold.

TOTAL CALORIES PER SERVING: 175   % OF CALORIES FROM FAT: 5%
PROTEIN: 5 gm   CARBOHYDRATES: 34 gm   FAT: 3 gm
CALCIUM: 47 mg   IRON: 1.5 mg   SODIUM: 53 mg   DIETARY FIBER: 2 gm

FOOD DEFINITIONS AND ORIGINS

ALMONDS are nuts found in the fruit of a small tree known as *Prunus amygdalus*. No one knows exactly where the almond originated, but *Prunus ulmifolia*, the wild species from China, contributed to our present day nut. When blended with water and strained, almonds make an excellent nut milk. Almonds are good sources of healthy oils.

APPLES are firm, rounded fruits of the tree *Pyrus malus*, which grows in temperate regions. There are about 7,500 different types of apples worldwide, including 2,500 varieties in the United States alone. The majority of commercially grown apple crops in this country consist of 18 to 25 varieties. "Delicious" is the most common. The skin of the apple is usually red, but may be yellow or green. Apples are high in fiber.

ARROWROOT is a fine white powdery substance that comes from a tropical plant and can be used to thicken gravies, soups, and fruit compotes. It also is called arrowroot starch, arrowroot flour, and arrowroot powder. It is used in much the same way that cornstarch is used and is found commonly in Asian shops.

AVOCADOS are oval or pear-shaped fruits that grow on a tropical American tree known as *Persea americana*. They have a leathery green or blackish skin, a large seed, and bland, yellowish-green edible pulp. Avocados are native to Central America. They are also called alligator pears. Avocados are good sources of healthy oils.

BANANAS are crescent-shaped fruits grown on several treelike tropical or subtropical plants of the genus *Musa*. The most widely cultivated banana grows on *Musa sapientum*, a plant which has long broad leaves and hanging clusters of fruit. The edible part of a banana consists of a white, pulpy flesh. The flesh is surrounded by a yellow or reddish skin, which can be peeled away easily. Bananas are high in potassium. They originated over 4,000 years ago in Malaysia.

BEETS are fleshy, dark red roots that are eaten as a vegetable. They grow on any of several widely cultivated plants of the genus *Beta*, especially *Beta vulgaris*. The leaves can be eaten as greens.

BELL PEPPERS are mild-flavored, bell-shaped fruits of the plant *Capisicum frutescens grossum*, which is native to Latin America. Bell peppers are red when ripe, but often are eaten when green. They are also called sweet peppers. Bell peppers are rich in vitamin C.

BLACK-EYED PEAS are the seeds of cowpeas. They are white with a black spot and look more like a bean than a pea. Black-eyed peas traditionally are eaten in the southeastern United States on New Year's Day. They are sometimes called "soul food." Both peas and beans are good sources of dietary fiber.

BLUEBERRIES are small berries that grow on any of several North American shrubs of the genus *Vaccinium*. The shrubs flower before producing berries. The fruit is blue, purplish, or blackish, and very sweet when ripe. Wild blueberry bushes can be found along hiking trails in the mountains. The berries produced on these bushes tend to be smaller and not as sweet.

BOK CHOY is an Oriental vegetable that is similar to, but milder in taste than, cabbage. Bok choy has snow-white stalks, a slightly bulbous base, and dark green leaves. Hong Kong farmers alone grow over twenty varieties of *Brassica chinensis*. In the United States four or five kinds are available. Bok choy sum or choy sum is almost identical to bok choy, but has yellow flowers. It is slightly smaller with narrower stalks. Bok choy sum also has green leaves, which are a shade lighter. Shanghai bok choy has spoon-shaped leaves and stems that are flatter than regular bok choy. Shanghai bok choy has light green leaves and is picked at a smaller size than bok choy. Taiwan bok choy is a yellowish green color and has broad delicate leaves that are almost lettuce-like in texture. Bok choy can be used in place of cabbage or even celery in some dishes.

BROCCOLI is the flower of the plant, *Brassica oleracea italica*. The plant is derived from wild cabbage. The flower is eaten as a vegetable before the green, tightly clustered buds have opened. Broccoli is high in vitamin C and a good source of calcium.

BULGUR is the bran and germ of wheat grain. It is also called cracked wheat. Bulgur is to the Middle East what rice is to the Orient and kasha is to Russia. It can be used in salads or in place of rice. Bulgur can be added to spaghetti sauce to thicken it.

CABBAGES are plants, *Brassica oleracea capitata*, which grow in temperate climates throughout the world. They have a short, thick stalk, and a large head formed by tightly overlapping green or reddish leaves. The Italians developed the popular savoy cabbage.

CANTALOUPES are a variety of melon known as *Cucumis melo cantalupensis*, which has ribbed fruit with a rough rind and an aromatic orange flesh. In the United States canteloupes are also known as muskmelons or *Cucumis melo reticulatus*.

CARROTS are the long, tapering yellow-orange roots of the widely cultivated plant, *Dacus carota sativa*. The plant has finely divided leaves and white flowers. This vegetable is native to the Near East and Central Asia. In its ancient form, the edible root was purple, not orange. Carrots are high in vitamin A.

CASHEWS are kidney-shaped nuts that grow on tropical evergreen trees known as *Anacardium occidentale*. Cashews actually are the seed of the cashew fruit, which is a fleshy, pear-shaped "apple." The seed (nut) hangs from the outside end of the fruit. The tree is native to coastal areas of northeastern Brazil. Cashews are the fifth leading nut crop in the world.

CAULIFLOWER is a compact whitish flower head of the plant *Brassica oleracea botrytis*. It is related to cabbage and broccoli and is derived from wild cabbage plants. Cauliflower is an excellent source of vitamin C.

CELERY is the stalk of the plant *Apium graveolens dulce*, which is native to Europe and Asia. Its small seeds, celery seeds, are used as seasoning. Celery is the third leading salad crop in the United States. It is derived from wild celery, which had more leaves.

CHICKPEAS are seeds. They grow on a bushy plant known as *Cicer arietenum* in the Mediterranean region and Central Asia. They also are called garbanzo beans. Eighty-seven percent of chickpeas are produced in India and Pakistan.

CHINESE BROCCOLI is an Oriental vegetable with smooth, round, green stems and has larger leaves than Western broccoli. The Latin name for Chinese broccoli is *Brassica alboglabra*. It is also called Chinese kale and *Gai lan* in Cantonese. Chinese broccoli has a cluster of white flowers on the stem and can be used in place of western broccoli in many dishes. Chinese broccoli is high in calcium.

CHINESE CABBAGE is the most important leafy vegetable of northern China. The Latin name for Chinese cabbage is *Brassica perkinensis*. It is also called napa cabbage, celery cabbage, *Hakusai* in Japanese, and *Wong nga bok choy* or *wong bok* in Cantonese. Chinese cabbage can be used in place of Western cabbage in most recipes.

COCONUT is the fruit of the coconut palm. The seed of the fruit is large, with a thick, hard shell that encloses edible white meat. The center of the seed is filled with a milky liquid. The liquid is known as coconut milk. Coconut can be eaten fresh or dried and grated. It is high in fat and should be used only in small quantities.

COLLARD GREENS are large, dark green leaves grown on a variety of the kale plant known as *Brassica oleracea acephala*. Collards are grown mostly in the southeastern United States. They are high in calcium.

CORN is a tall, widely cultivated cereal plant known as *Zea mays*. The plant bears seeds or kernels on large ears. There are several different varieties of corn. Corn is indigenous to the United States and is sometimes called Indian corn or maize. In England, "corn" refers to wheat; in Scotland and Ireland, "corn" refers to oats.

CORNMEAL can be white or yellow. White cornmeal is milled from white corn and yellow cornmeal is milled from yellow corn. Cornmeal is more coarse in texture than flour. It can be used in baking or as a hot cereal.

CUCUMBERS are cylindrical fruits which grow on the vine known as *Cucumis sativus*. The fruit has a hard green rind and white succulent flesh. China is the largest producer of cucumbers.

DATES are sweet, oblong fruits of the date palm. They contain a narrow hard seed. Unlike most fruits, dates do not contain any vitamin C. Dates grow on what is called the Tree of Life and grew in the Holy Land at least 8,000 years ago. They grow in clusters of up to 200 dates weighing up to 25 pounds. They rank among the top twenty fruits of the world. Today, Egypt is the largest producer of dates.

EGGPLANT is an ovoid fruit which has a glossy, dark, purple skin. It grows on the tropical Old World plant *Solanum melongena*. When cooked, eggplant is eaten as a vegetable. Eggplants are used widely in Greek, Italian, and Middle Eastern cooking. They are also known as aubergines.

FAVA BEANS resemble lima beans, but are slightly larger. Fava beans also are known as horse beans and broad beans. This legume is referred to in the Bible and was consumed throughout the Old World. Fava beans are native to northern Africa and the eastern Mediterranean region. The Chinese used fava beans 5,000 years ago. Today, China is the largest producer of fava beans.

GARDEN PEAS are seeds found in an elongated green pod. The pods grow on a climbing vine known as *Pisum sativum*, which is found in all temperate zones. Peas are among the top ten vegetable crops grown in the world. They were first used by the Chinese in 2000 BCE. Peas are mentioned in the Bible and for many years were used in the dry form only.

GARLIC is the bulb of the plant *Allium sativum*. It has a strong, distinctive flavor and odor. Garlic consists of separate cloves and is used as a seasoning. It is a perennial herb native to Central Asia.

KALE is the ruffled or crinkled leaf of a variety of cabbage called *Brassica oleracea acephala*. The leaves do not form a tight head. Kale is high in calcium.

KIDNEY BEANS are known as *Phaseolus vulgaris*. They are native to Mexico and Peru and are cultivated for their seeds. They are reddish brown in color.

LEMONS are small, yellow, egg-shaped citrus fruits that grow on a spiny tree. They have an aromatic rind and acidic, juicy pulp. Lemons are native to Southeast Asia. In the United States, lemons are the sixth leading fruit crop. Worldwide, Italy is the largest producer of lemons. Lemons and all other citrus fruits are excellent sources of vitamin C.

LENTILS are seeds which grow in pods on a leguminous plant known as *Lens esculenta* or *Lens culinaris.* There are two varieties of lentils. Brown lentils were cultivated by the ancient Egyptians and Greeks. They grow two per small pod and are greenish brown in color. Red lentils are orange-red in color and cook more quickly because they are split in half when dried. Lentils are a good source of vitamin B6.

MILLET is the white seed of the plant, *Panicum miliaceium.* Globally, eighty-five percent of the millet crop is used for food. Millions of people in India, Africa, China, and parts of the Soviet Union depend on millet for seventy percent or more of their caloric intake. In North America, millet, which is grown as a grass, is used mostly for hay. Ninety-four percent of millet is produced in Asia and Africa. China alone produces forty-seven percent.

MOLASSES is a thick dark syrup that is produced when sugarcane juice is boiled down and the raw sugar is extracted. Blackstrap molasses results from the third stage of refining white sugar. Blackstrap molasses is high in iron and calcium.

MUSHROOMS are fleshy fungi of the class *Basidiomycetes.* Some mushrooms are edible, while others are poisonous and should not be consumed. There are about 38,000 types of mushrooms worldwide. The most common mushroom found in the United States has a white umbrella-shaped cap borne on a stalk. Mushrooms are a good source of the B vitamin riboflavin.

OATS are seeds that grow on any of several grasses of the genus *Avena*, especially *Avena sativa*. Wild stocks of oats first grew in Asia. Oats rank sixth among cereal grains. Today the Soviet Union is the largest producer of oats.

OKRA is a mucilaginous green pod that grows on the tall tropical and semitropical plant known as *Hibiscus esculentus*. Okra is native to Africa and also is known as gumbo.

ONIONS are round edible bulbs composed of tight, concentric layers, which have a pungent odor and taste. The onion plant, *Allium cepa*, is cultivated worldwide as a vegetable. Onions are native to the central part of Asia between Iran and Pakistan and toward southern Russia.

ORANGES are round fruits with a yellowish-red rind and a sectioned pulpy interior. Oranges have a sweet acid juice and are high in vitamin C. Oranges grow on several evergreen trees of the genus *Citrus*, cultivated in tropical and subtropical regions. The trees have fragrant white flowers. There are different types of oranges, including *Citrus aurantium*, Seville or sour orange. There also is *Citrus sinensis*, the sweet orange which is native to the area between South China and Indochina. Twenty-nine percent of oranges worldwide are grown in the United States. Florida is the leading producer.

PAPAYAS are large yellow fruits native to Central America. They grow on the *Carica papaya*, a tropical American evergreen.

PEACHES are single-seeded fruits with a red-tinted, yellow skin and yellow flesh. Peaches are soft and juicy when ripe. Peach classification is based on how difficult it is to remove the pit. The most common varieties are known as freestone and clingstone. Peaches grow on the *Pronus persica* tree. They were eaten in China over 4,000 years ago. The peach found its way to Persia (Iran) and is known there as the Persian Apple. Today, the United States and Italy are the leading producers of peaches.

PEANUTS grow on a vine known as *Arachis hupogaea*, which is native to tropical America and widely cultivated in semi-tropical regions. The tree has yellow flowers. The stalks bend over and the seed pod, which contains the peanuts, grows and ripens underground. The peanut is also called a groundnut. It evolved thousands of years ago in South America. Today, eighty percent of all peanuts are produced in Africa and Asia, especially in India.

PEARS are large fruits with round bottoms that taper inward toward the stem. Some pears are completely round. Pears are covered with a smooth yellow, russet, or red skin when ripe. There are several hundred varieties of pears. Pears are indigenous to western Asia. The Bartlett pear is the most commonly found pear in the United States. Today, Italy is the largest producer of pears. Pears are closely related to the apple and are a good source of fiber. Pears can be eaten fresh, baked, or cooked and can be prepared much the same way that apples are.

PINE NUTS are the seeds of certain pine trees, such as the pinon. The seeds are beige in color.

PINEAPPLES are large fleshy fruits native to South America. They grow on a tropical American plant known as *Ananas comosus*, which has large, swordlike leaves. The pineapple is thought to have originated in Brazil. Today, China is the leading producer of pineapples.

PINTO BEANS are a form of the common string bean that has mottled seeds. They are grown chiefly in the southwestern United States.

POTATOES are starchy tubers that come from the plant *Solanum tubersosum*, which is native to South America. Potato skins are yellow, brown, or red in color. The potato is also called the Irish potato and the white potato. Potatoes were first cultivated between four and seven thousand years ago in the Andes Mountains of Bolivia and Peru. Potatoes are not related to sweet potatoes or yams. Potatoes are good sources of potassium.

PRUNES are dried plums. They look like over-sized, dark raisins. Prunes are an excellent source of iron and fiber.

RAISINS are dried sweet grapes of several varieties and are dried either in the sun or artificially. Their name comes from the Latin word *racemus*, meaning cluster of grapes or berries. Raisins have been enjoyed since ancient times. Today, California is the largest producer of these high-fiber snacks.

RICE is the starchy seed of a cereal grass known as *Oryza sativa*, cultivated extensively in warm climates. Rice is a staple food throughout the world. Ninety-four percent is produced in the Orient. Rice provides a majority of the food for over half of humanity.

SCALLIONS are green in color with a tiny white bulb. They are young onions which are harvested before the bulb enlarges.

SEITAN (pronounced say-tan) is wheat gluten that has been cooked in soy sauce. It is commonly eaten in China, Korea, Russia, and the Middle East. To make seitan, water is added to wheat flour. The mixture is kneaded to a consistency similar to that of bread dough. The bran and starch then are rinsed repeatedly out of the dough until only the gluten remains. The gluten then is simmered in a broth. Asian stores carry wheat gluten. They call it *mien ching* or *yu mien ching*. The broth seitan is simmered in is high in sodium.

SPINACH is the succulent green leaf of the widely cultivated plant *Spinacia oleracea*. It is native to Asia. The United States, the Netherlands, and Scandinavia are the major producers of spinach. Spinach and several other leafy green vegetables are good sources of vitamin A.

SPLIT PEAS are green or yellow peas that have been shelled, dried, and split. They are especially used in soups and stews. Split peas contain dietary fiber and protein.

SQUASH is a fleshy fruit with a hard rind which grows on any of a variety of plants of the genus *Cucurbita*. Its wild ancestors are native to the area between Mexico and Guatemala. Today, China is the largest producer of squash. There are many popular varieties of squash available in the United States. Summer squashes such as yellow squash and zucchini are soft and watery. Winter squashes such as acorn squash, butternut squash, and vegetable spaghetti, are mature, hard skinned, and have a mildly flavored, finely-grained flesh.

STRAWBERRIES are the world's leading berry-type fruit. The strawberry is a small, red fruit that is an excellent source of vitamin C. When ripe, it is extremely sweet. Strawberry seeds grow on the outside of the fruit; thus, in a botanical sense, they are really not berries. Today, the United States is the largest producer of strawberries.

STRING BEANS are narrow green pods also known as green beans or snap beans. If the pod is yellow it is known as a wax bean. These beans grow on the climbing plant called *Phaseolus vulgaris*.

TEMPEH (pronounced tem-pay) is a staple in Indonesia produced by fermenting pre-soaked and cooked soybeans and sometimes a grain with a culture called rhizopus. The soybeans are hulled before being cooked and inoculated with a starter culture grown on hibiscus leaves. The fermentation process binds the beans together and gives them flavor. Tempeh is an excellent source of protein. If gray or black spots appear on the tempeh, it is the result of natural sporulation and not indicative of spoilage. Tempeh can be fried in a little oil, steamed, boiled, or baked. It is often mixed with grains and vegetables in casseroles.

TOFU, also known as bean curd and soy cheese, is made from soy milk in a similar fashion to the way cheese is made from milk. The soy milk is heated until it boils, a curdling agent is added, and then the curds are separated from the whey. The curds are pressed together to form blocks of tofu. Tofu can be bought in several forms including soft, which is great for dips and dressings, and firm, which is good for stews, etc. Tofu was made originally in China, where it is called *dou-fu*, from a variety of beans and peas. In fact, tofu is still made from mung beans in some places. Tofu has grown in popularity in the United States and can be found in most supermarkets.

TOMATOES are fruits that are usually red in color, although yellow and orange varieties do exist. They grow on the plant *Lycoperscion esculentum* which is native to South America. Contemporary tomatoes derive from their primitive ancestor, the cherry tomato, which first grew in the Peru-Ecuador area. Today, the United States is the largest producer of this vitamin C-rich fruit.

UNBLEACHED WHITE FLOUR is a variety of flour that has had most of the bran and germ removed and is not a whole grain. However, it has not been bleached with chlorides and is often grown organically. Unbleached white flour is not as nutritious as whole wheat flour, but is better than bleached flour.

WATER CHESTNUTS are corms, underwater stem tips, from which a kind of water grass sprouts. Water chestnuts have a sweet crispness like coconut and are off-white in color. They are popular in Asian cooking and are called *ma tai* in the Cantonese dialect of Chinese.

WHOLE WHEAT PASTRY FLOUR is made from soft winter wheat and is lower in gluten than flour derived from hard wheat. Whole wheat pastry flour is used to make baked goods that are tender and finely textured. It often is not stoneground, but rather milled in a hammer mill that reduces the soft white or soft red wheat to small particles. Whole wheat pastry flour is not as coarse in texture as whole wheat flour.

ZUCCHINI is a variety of squash that is elongated and has a smooth, thin, dark green rind.

HERBS AND SPICES

ALLSPICE tastes like a combination of cloves, cinnamon, and nutmeg. It comes from the purple, pear-sized fruit of the tree, *Pimenta officinalis*. Most allspice is produced in Jamaica.

CARAWAY SEEDS are pungent aromatic seeds of the *Carum carvi* plant. This plant has finely divided leaves and clusters of small white flowers. Caraway seeds are used in baking and cooking. Most of the caraway seeds found in the United States are imported from the Netherlands.

CAYENNE PEPPER is a condiment made from the pungent fruit of a variety of the plant known as *Capsicum frutescens*. It is also called cayenne or red pepper. Cayenne pepper is made by grinding dried chili peppers. The chili peppers are native to the area around the Cayenne River in French Guiana. Cayenne pepper should be used sparingly because it is a very hot spice.

CHILI is the pungent fruit of several varieties of a woody plant known as *Capsicum frutescens*. The powdered form is made by grinding the fruit after it has been dried. Chili powder is very high in vitamin A.

CINNAMON is the yellowish-brown bark of one of two trees, *Cinnamomum zeylanicum* or *Cinnamomum lourer*. The bark is dried, and often ground. Cinnamon is native to Ceylon (Sri Lanka), India, and Malaysia.

CORIANDER is the dried fruit of the small annual plant, *Coriandrum sativum*, which is native to the Mediterranean region. It is usually imported from Morocco.

CUMIN is the aromatic seed of an Old World plant known as *Cuminum cyminum*. The plant has finely divided leaves and small white pinkish flowers. Often, the seeds are ground into a powdered form. Cumin has been used as a spice since Biblical times.

CURRY is a mixture of spices that originated in India and is used often in Indian dishes, including sauces and relishes.

DILL is the leaf or seed of an aromatic herb known as *Anethum graveolens*. The plant has finely dissected leaves and small yellow flowers. It is native to southwestern Asia.

GINGER is the pungent, aromatic, rootstock of the plant *Zingiber officinale*, found in tropical Asia. It has yellowish-green flowers. It often is dried and powdered to be used as a flavoring or as a sweetmeat in a sugared form. Ginger often is used in Chinese cooking.

MARJORAM is the leaf of an aromatic plant known as *Majorana hortensis*. The plant has small purplish-white flowers. Marjoram is also called sweet marjoram. It is native to West Asia and the Mediterranean region. Marjoram is a perennial herb belonging to the mint family.

MINT originated in the Old World and grows on various plants of the genus *Mentha*, characteristically having aromatic foliage and flowers. There are about 3,200 different types of mint.

MUSTARD is a tiny yellowish-brown, round seed that often is ground into a powder or paste. It grows on any of various plants of the genus *Brassica*, native to Europe and Asia. The plant has four-petaled, yellow flowers and slender pods.

NUTMEG is derived from the hard aromatic seeds of the evergreen tree known as *Myristica fragrans*, native to the East Indies and cultivated elsewhere in the tropics. Nutmeg is used as a spice when grated or ground.

OREGANO is an herb made from the dried leaves of a species of marjoram known as *Origanum vulgare*. It is popular in Italian cuisine.

PAPRIKA is a mild, powdered seasoning made from the dried pods of sweet red peppers. Paprika is dark, vivid, reddish-orange in color. It is the national spice of Hungary and used extensively in Spanish cooking.

PARSLEY is the dried, curled leaf of the cultivated herb *Petroselinum*. Parsley is used both as a seasoning and as a garnish. It originated in the Mediterranean area and is an excellent source of vitamins A and C. Parsley is also rich in iron.

PEPPER is the dried, berrylike, blackish fruit of the plant *Piper nigrum*, which is a woody vine of the East Indies. Pepper is a pungent spice. It is called black pepper when the whole berry is ground and white pepper when the shell has been removed before grinding.

SESAME SEEDS come from the plant *Sesamum indicum*, which is grown mostly in India, as well as China and Sudan. Sesame seeds are beige in color and sometimes ground to form sesame butter or tahini.

SWEET BASIL is the herb, *Ocimum basilicum*, which is native to the Old World. It consists of spikes of small white flowers and aromatic leaves, which are used as seasoning. Sweet basil originally came from India and Iran.

TARRAGON is the leaf of the herb known as *Artemisia dracunculus*, which is native to Europe and Asia. It is used both in its fresh and dried form. Tarragon originated in Siberia. There are two varieties. One is Russian and the other is French. In the United States, the French variety is used more often.

THYME is the leaf of several aromatic herbs or low shrubs of the genus *Thymus*, especially *Thymus vulgaris*, which is found in southern Europe near the mountains along the Riviera. The plant has small purplish flowers and the leaves are used as seasoning.

TURMERIC is the powdered rootstock from the *Curcuma longa* plant of India. It is used as a condiment and as a yellow dye. Turmeric is native to southeastern Asia and is in the same family as ginger. Turmeric is used to give mustard its yellow color.

VEGAN NUTRITION

INTRODUCTION

Eating is one of the most basic acts we perform and it is something the majority of people don't even think about! Many factors influence the foods we select — cost, availability, taste, appearance, religious or ethical principles, and so forth. Nutrition also influences food choices. For example, you may select whole-wheat bread over white bread; fresh fruit over sweetened, canned fruit; and a baked potato over French fries.

Can a vegan diet, chosen for health, environmental, ethical, or other reasons, meet nutritional needs? Absolutely! The key to a nutritionally sound vegan diet is variety. Just as you would worry about a friend who only ate hamburgers, you should also worry about a friend who only eats potato chips and salad. A healthy and varied vegan diet includes fruits, vegetables, plenty of leafy greens, whole grain products, nuts, seeds, and legumes. It's that easy.

In fact, if you stopped reading right now and went out and ate a wide variety of foods, chances are good that you would have a nutritionally adequate diet. A vegan diet requires no more careful planning than does a meat-centered diet. And, in fact, since meat-eaters are more likely than are vegetarians to die of diet-related diseases like heart attacks, certain cancers, and hypertension, perhaps meat-eating Americans should spend more time properly planning their diets.

We are writing this section on vegan nutrition to explain how a vegan diet can meet nutritional needs. You may use the facts which we present for reassurance, to improve your diet, or to share with others.

To simplify matters, the discussion of each nutrient will feature a summary paragraph, in bold type, which can be used to provide a quick idea of the most important facts about that nutrient. The end of this section features a glossary of nutrition-related terms.

NUTRITION IS A SCIENCE

Summary: Epidemiological, clinical, and laboratory studies are all used in nutrition research. Most scientists believe each type of study has its strengths and limitations. Studies are the basis of nutritional recommendations, so recommendations change as knowledge about nutritional requirements is acquired.

Nutrition is a science, just as chemistry, biology, and physics are sciences. Since nutrition is a science, it involves research and the use of scientific methods to answer questions. The questions which nutrition researchers ask are often about which foods and how much of those foods people should eat. Research studies are designed to answer specific questions. Studies may differ in their design and in the method they use to answer a question.

For example, to answer the question "What can I eat to keep from getting cancer?" one scientist might collect information on the diets of groups of people for many years and see which people got cancer and which didn't. The scientist would then compare the diets of these two groups. Another scientist might conduct an intervention study where people are randomly assigned to either follow or not follow a certain diet or to use or not use a certain food or supplement. The scientist would then determine the effect of the intervention on the subjects' health. A third scientist might use cells or tissues or animals to evaluate the effects of a certain nutrient on cancer occurrence.

These types of studies are examples of epidemiological, clinical, and laboratory studies, respectively. Most scientists see advantages and disadvantages with each type of study.

Epidemiology is the study of populations. Often in epidemiological studies, people are asked to describe their diets, either current or past. The amounts of different substances in their diets are then correlated with incidence of certain diseases or conditions. Epidemiological studies may also measure the levels of substances such as vitamins or minerals in blood or urine and attempt to correlate these levels with diet or health.

The major strength of epidemiological studies is that they are able to look at large groups of people for a long period of time. People from more than one region or more than one country can be included. People of different ages, genders, and ethnic origins can be studied. Epidemiological studies look at people, so the results of these studies are directly applicable to humans and do not have to be extrapolated from cells or animals.

On the other hand, there are limitations to epidemiological studies, particularly those that are based on people's descriptions of what they eat. There are several different tools available to collect this information, but all have some limitations. They all rely on the subjects to describe accurately what they eat. This is difficult for many people. If you were a subject in a nutrition study, and you were asked to tell an investigator everything that you ate or drank yesterday, would you remember everything? Would you know how much of each food you had eaten? And how representative of your "typical" diet would that one day's intake be? Besides the limitations due to inaccurate reporting of subjects, another limitation is that investigators are unable to know all the factors affecting their subjects. For example, subjects may have a high rate of cancer because of exposure to radiation, not due to dietary factors at all.

Clinical studies also use human subjects, but these studies are often smaller than epidemiological studies. They modify people's diets or activity levels and then study the effects of these changes. These studies are also called randomized trials or intervention studies.

As with epidemiological studies, an advantage of clinical studies is that they use human subjects so the results of these studies are directly applicable to humans. An additional strength of clinical studies is that they are more controlled. Often in a clinical study, subjects are housed in a metabolic unit, where all food is provided and activity is closely monitored. This allows investigators to know exactly what is going on with their subjects.

A drawback of this type of study is that very few people live in a controlled setting so the results of these studies may not be the same as those in real life. Also, people are unwilling to live in a metabolic ward for a long time. If a scientist is trying to answer a question about something that takes many years to occur, the results of a clinical study may not be helpful.

Laboratory studies are used because they allow investigators to have more control than is possible in human studies. These studies are often less expensive than studies using human subjects. However, results of these studies can only provide preliminary information. Animals, tissues, and cells are not a substitute for humans. In addition, many people see moral reasons not to experiment on animals.

Often we are faced with newspaper headlines like "Coffee Drinking Leads to Pancreatic Cancer" or "Vegans Have a Deficiency of Vitamin X." These are frequently based on the result of one study. When you read a report like this or hear the latest nutrition news on radio or television, consider the strengths and limitations of each type of nutrition study. Usually, one study is not enough to answer a large question in an area as complex as nutrition.

Normally, when a controversial study is published, other scientists begin to do experiments to see if they can get similar results. If several scientists, using different methods, come to similar conclusions, more faith can be placed in their results.

Often the results of a variety of studies are used to make nutritional recommendations. Recommendations made by groups such as the National Academy of Sciences, the Dietary Guidelines Advisory Committee, the Academy of Nutrition and Dietetics (formerly known as the American Dietetic Association), the American Cancer Society, and the American Heart Association are usually made by a committee of scientists who have conducted a thorough review of the existing information on the subject. Recommendations change due to new information and to new ways of looking at previously collected information.

We do know a lot about nutrition and our knowledge base is growing daily. Nutrition studies can be used to make recommendations about what people should eat to achieve good health. In this nutrition section, the results of scientific studies will be used to make recommendations specifically aimed at people following vegan diets.

RECOMMENDATIONS FOR VEGANS

Summary: A vegan diet conforms to recommendations made to reduce the risk of the major chronic diseases such as heart disease and cancer. The long-term quality of an individual's diet should be used to assess its nutritional adequacy. The Dietary Reference Intakes (DRIs) are commonly used to make recommendations for nutrient intake.

What do the various government agencies and other groups that make recommendations about the nation's health have to say about vegan diets? In some cases very positive statements are made about vegetarian and sometimes about vegan diets. Often, careful reading between the lines, even if no mention is made of vegetarianism, evokes the idea that diets similar to those followed by many American vegans are being recommended by governmental and scientific groups.

The latest edition of Dietary Guidelines for Americans was issued in 2010 (1). The Dietary Guidelines are a statement of current federal policy on the role of dietary factors in health promotion and disease prevention. The Departments of Agriculture (USDA) and Health and Human Services issue these guidelines.

The text of the Dietary Guidelines for Americans, 2010 states, "In prospective studies of adults, compared to non-vegetarian eating patterns, vegetarian-style eating patterns have been associated with improved health outcomes—lower levels of obesity, a reduced risk of cardiovascular disease, and lower total mortality. Several clinical trials have documented that vegetarian eating patterns lower blood pressure (1)." The Guidelines go on to say, "On average, vegetarians consume a lower proportion of calories from fat (particularly saturated fatty acids); fewer overall calories; and more fiber, potassium, and vitamin C than do non-vegetarians. Vegetarians generally have a lower body mass index. These characteristics and other lifestyle factors associated with a vegetarian diet may contribute to the positive health outcomes that have been identified among vegetarians (1)." Vegan eating patterns are included in the Guidelines. The vegan "dairy" group includes calcium-fortified beverages and foods commonly used as substitutes for milk and milk products. The protein foods group includes beans, peas, soy products, nuts, and seeds.

All Americans are reminded to eat more vegetables, fruits, beans and peas, and whole grains, and to choose a diet low in saturated fats, *trans* fats, and cholesterol. Vegan diets that stress whole grains, legumes, vegetables, and fruits and avoid foods of animal origin are generally low in total fat, low in saturated fat, high in complex carbohydrates and fiber, and absolutely free of cholesterol.

The Academy of Nutrition and Dietetics states, "Appropriately planned vegetarian diets, including total vegetarian or vegan diets, are healthful, nutritionally adequate, and may provide health benefits in the prevention and treatment of certain diseases" (2). They go on to endorse well-planned vegan diets as being appropriate for all stages of the life cycle including pregnancy and lactation, and for infants, children, and adolescents.

The website for the newly designed MyPlate food guide provides specific tips for vegetarians including choosing beans, nuts, and peas as protein sources and using calcium-fortified soy milk (3). The Vegetarian Resource Group has developed a vegan version of MyPlate (see centerfold of this book). An alternative tool for vegan meal planning can be found on page 198.

The American Institute for Cancer Research and the World Cancer Research Fund developed a series of recommendations for the general public worldwide. These include "Choose predominantly plant-based diets rich in a variety of vegetables and fruits, legumes, and minimally processed starchy staple foods. Eat 15-30 ounces or five or more servings a day of a variety of vegetables and fruits, all year round. Eat 20-30 ounces or more than seven servings a day of a variety of grains, legumes, roots, tubers, and plantains. Prefer minimally processed foods. Limit consumption of refined sugar" (4). These recommendations are certainly consistent with a vegan diet.

Similarly, the American Heart Association calls for a diet low in saturated fat and cholesterol to reduce the risk of heart disease (5). Again, this is certainly in line with a vegan diet.

Dietary Reference Intakes

The Dietary Reference Intake Committee of the National Academy of

Science's Institute of Medicine reviews all available information and develops recommendations for the amounts of essential nutrients needed by Americans. Since nutrition is a rapidly changing field, recommendations do change. This committee produces recommendations that are commonly called the Recommended Dietary Allowances (RDAs); Adequate Intakes (AIs) are issued for nutrients where the RDA cannot be determined.

The RDAs are defined as "the average daily dietary intake level that is sufficient to meet the nutrient requirement of nearly all healthy individuals in a particular life stage and gender group" (6). Since there is a margin of safety, if your diet does not meet the RDA for every nutrient, every day, you should not be concerned. It is more important to consider the quality of your diet over time.

Generally, when making recommendations for the amounts of nutrients needed for vegans, we will refer to the DRIs. In some instances, we will turn to the recommendations of international bodies such as the World Health Organization (WHO) for a different perspective.

References

1. U.S. Department of Agriculture and U.S. Department of Health and Human Services. *Dietary Guidelines for Americans, 2010.* 7th Edition, Washington, DC: U.S. Government Printing Office, 2010.

2. Craig WJ, Mangels AR. Position of The American Dietetic Association: Vegetarian Diets. *J Am Diet Assoc* 2009;109:1266-82.

3. USDA. Vegetarian Diets. http://www.choosemyplate.gov/tipsresources /vegetarian_diets.html. Accessed June 8, 2011.

4. World Cancer Research Fund/AICR. *Food, Nutrition, Physical Activity, and the Prevention of Cancer: a Global Perspective.* Washington, DC:AICR, 2007.

5. Lichtenstein AH, Appel LJ, Brands M, et al. American Heart Association Nutrition Committee, Diet and Lifestyle Recommendations Revision 2006: A Scientific Statement from the American Heart Association Nutrition Committee. *Circulation.* 2006;114:82–96.

6. Institute of Medicine. *Dietary Reference Intakes for Energy, Carbohydrate, Fiber, Fat, Fatty Acids, Cholesterol, Protein, and Amino Acids.* Washington, DC: National Academy Press, 2002.

CALORIES, WEIGHT GAIN, AND WEIGHT LOSS

Summary: Protein, fat, and carbohydrates all provide energy in the form of calories. Fat is the most concentrated source of calories. To lose weight, eat less and exercise more. To gain weight, eat more.

In a discussion of nutrition, the words "calories" and "energy" are interchangeable. That's because a calorie is a measure of the amount of energy provided by a food. Adequate energy is essential. We need enough calories (that is, energy) to function every day. If enough food (calories) is not eaten, the body will break down both muscle protein and fat, wounds will not heal, children will not grow, and individuals of any age will eventually become ill and die.

There is an easy way to see whether or not your diet contains enough calories. Look at your weight. Normally, non-pregnant adults should be neither losing nor gaining weight. Caloric intake should equal energy output. In other words, the calories (energy) from foods you eat should be approximately the same as the calories you "burn up" in activity. If you are losing weight unintentionally, you are probably not taking in enough calories. Similarly, if you are gaining weight, you are taking in more calories than you expend.

At this time, more than 2 out of 3 adults in the United States are significantly overweight (1). Many factors including our more sedentary lifestyles, food marketing and advertising, and the easy availability of food have been identified as contributing to the problem. Health risks associated with obesity include increased risk of heart disease, high blood pressure, gallbladder disease, type 2 diabetes, and some kinds of cancer.

Vegans as a group tend to be lean. In other words, a vegan has a better chance of not being overweight than a non-vegetarian (2). This may be because vegan diets are usually higher in fiber. Fiber, found in whole grains, dried beans, fruits, and vegetables, helps to make us feel full. This feeling of satiety may help us to stop eating before we overeat.

For those vegans who are trying to lose weight, a reduction in dietary fat may be an easy way to cut calories, especially if your diet is high in fatty foods like oils, salad dressings, margarine, nuts, and nut butters. Fats provide a concentrated source of calories; often a small amount of high-fat food can have more calories than you might expect. For instance, a quarter cup of shelled peanuts has about 200 calories. If you ate salad greens (without dressing), you'd have to eat 40 cups to get 200 calories. While being aware of high-fat foods is important for weight loss, at the end of the day, it's your total calorie intake and energy expenditure that determine whether you lose weight, gain weight, or stay at the same weight. In addition to reducing calorie intake, increased activity is also an important component of weight reduction (3).

Bulky foods, as are commonly eaten on vegan diets, can make it difficult for some young children or pregnant women to gain weight. Individuals in these groups can become full before getting the calories they need. For those who need to increase weight, grow, or stop losing weight, it is sometimes necessary to increase the fat and thereby increase the number of calories in the diet. Since fat is a more concentrated source of calories than either carbohydrate or protein, moderate use of higher fat foods such as nuts, seeds, avocados, nut butters (e.g., peanut butter, almond butter) and seed butters (e.g., tahini which is also called sesame butter), and soy products can help with weight gain. Vegans, especially children and others trying to gain weight, should eat small meals or snacks throughout the day.

References

1. Flegal KM, Carroll MO, Kit BK, Ogden CL. Prevalence of obesity and trends in the distribution of body mass index among US adults, 1999-2010. *JAMA* 2012;307:491-7.

2. Spencer EA, Appleby PN, Davey GK, Key TJ. Diet and body mass index in 38000 EPIC-Oxford meat-eaters, fish-eaters, vegetarians and vegans. *Int J Obes Relat Metab Disord.* 2003;27:728-34.

3. U.S. Department of Agriculture and U.S. Department of Health and Human Services. *Dietary Guidelines for Americans, 2010.* 7th edition, Washington, DC: U.S. Government Printing Office, 2010.

PROTEIN

Summary: It is easy for a vegan diet to meet recommendations for protein, as long as calorie intake is adequate. Strict protein combining is not necessary; it is more important to eat a varied diet throughout the day.

Some Americans are obsessed with protein. Vegans are bombarded with questions about where they get their protein. Athletes used to eat thick steaks before competition because they thought it would improve their performance. Protein supplements are sold at health food stores. This concern about protein is misplaced. Although protein is certainly an essential nutrient which plays many key roles in the way our bodies function, we do not need huge quantities of it. Only about one calorie out of every 10 we take in needs to come from protein. Vegan athletes, especially in the early stages of training, may have higher protein needs than vegans who exercise moderately or who are not active. Vegan athletes' protein needs can range from 0.36 to 0.86 grams of protein per pound (2). Protein supplements are not needed to achieve even the highest level of protein intake.

How much protein do we need? The RDA recommends that we take in 0.8 grams of protein for every kilogram that we weigh (or about 0.36 grams of protein per pound that we weigh) (1). This recommendation includes a generous safety factor for most people. When we make a few adjustments to account for some plant proteins being digested somewhat differently from animal proteins and for the amino acid mix in some plant proteins, we arrive at a level of 0.9 gram of protein per kilogram body weight (0.41 grams per pound). If we do a few calculations we see that the protein recommendation for vegans amounts to close to 10% of calories coming from protein. [For example, a vegan male weighing 174 pounds could have a calorie requirement of 2,600 calories. His protein needs are calculated as 174 pounds x 0.41 g/pound = 71 grams of protein. 71 grams of protein x 4 calories/gram of protein = 284 calories from protein. 284 divided by 2,600 calories = 10.9% of calories from protein.] If we look at what vegans are eating, we find that, typically, between 10-12% of calories come from protein (3). This contrasts with the protein intake of non-vegetarians, which is close to 14-18% of calories.

So, in the United States it appears that vegan diets are commonly lower in protein than standard American diets. Remember, though, with protein, more (than the RDA) is not necessarily better. There do not appear to be health advantages to consuming a high protein diet. Diets that are high in protein may even increase the risk of osteoporosis (4) and kidney disease (5).

Table 1: Sample Menus Showing How Easy It Is To Meet Protein Needs

		Protein (grams)
Breakfast:	1 cup Oatmeal	6
	1 cup Soy Milk	7
	1 medium Bagel	10
Lunch:	2 slices Whole Wheat Bread	7
	1 cup Vegetarian Baked Beans	12
Dinner:	5 oz firm Tofu	12
	1 cup cooked Broccoli	4
	1 cup cooked Brown Rice	5
	2 Tbsp Almonds	4
Snack:	2 Tbsp Peanut Butter	8
	6 Crackers	2
TOTAL		77 grams
Protein Recommendation for Male Vegan		63 grams

[based on 0.9 gram of protein per kilogram body weight for 70 kilogram (154 pound) male]

Breakfast:	2 slices Whole Wheat Toast	7
	2 Tbsp Peanut Butter	8
Lunch:	6 oz Soy Yogurt	6
	2 Tbsp Almonds	4
	1 medium Baked Potato	3
Dinner:	1 cup cooked Lentils	18
	1 cup cooked Bulgur	6
Snack:	1 cup Soy Milk	7
TOTAL		59 grams
Protein Recommendation for Female Vegan		52 grams

[based on 0.9 gram of protein per kilogram body weight for 57.5 kilogram (126 pound) female]

Additional food should be added to these menus to provide adequate calories and to meet requirements for nutrients besides protein.

Table 2 shows the amount of protein in various vegan foods and also the number of grams of protein per 100 calories. To meet protein recommendations, the typical moderately active adult male vegan needs only 2.2 to 2.6 grams of protein per 100 calories and the typical moderately active adult female vegan needs only 2.3 to 2.8 grams of protein per 100 calories. These recommendations can be easily met from vegan sources.

Table 2: Protein Content of Selected Vegan Foods

FOOD	AMOUNT	PROTEIN (gm)	PROTEIN (gm/100 cal)
Tempeh	1 cup	31	9.6
Soybeans, cooked	1 cup	29	9.6
Seitan	3 ounces	21	17.5
Lentils, cooked	1 cup	18	7.8
Black beans, cooked	1 cup	15	6.7
Kidney beans, cooked	1 cup	15	6.8
Chickpeas, cooked	1 cup	15	5.4
Pinto beans, cooked	1 cup	15	6.3
Lima beans, cooked	1 cup	15	6.8
Black-eyed peas, cooked	1 cup	13	6.7
Veggie burger	1 patty	13	18.6
Veggie baked beans	1 cup	12	5.0
Tofu, firm	4 ounces	11	10.6
Tofu, regular	4 ounces	10	10.7

Table 2 continued

FOOD	AMOUNT	PROTEIN (gm)	PROTEIN (gm/100 cal)
Bagel	1 med. (3.5 oz)	10	3.9
Quinoa, cooked	1 cup	8	3.7
Peas, cooked	1 cup	8	6.6
Textured Vegetable Protein (TVP), cooked	1/2 cup	8	15.0
Peanut butter	2 Tbsp	8	4.1
Veggie dog	1 link	8	13.3
Spaghetti, cooked	1 cup	8	3.7
Almonds	1/4 cup	8	3.7
Soy milk, commercial, plain	1 cup	7	7.0
Whole wheat bread	2 slices	7	5.2
Almond butter	2 Tbsp	7	3.4
Soy yogurt, plain	8 ounces	6	4.0
Bulgur, cooked	1 cup	6	3.7
Sunflower seeds	1/4 cup	6	3.3
Cashews	1/4 cup	5	2.7
Spinach, cooked	1 cup	5	13.0
Broccoli, cooked	1 cup	4	6.7

Sources: USDA Nutrient Database for Standard Reference, Release 24, 2011 and manufacturers' information.

The recommendation for protein for adult male vegans is around 63 grams per day; for adult female vegans it is around 52 grams per day.

It is very easy for a vegan diet to meet the recommendations for protein. Nearly all vegetables, beans, grains, nuts, and seeds contain some, and often much, protein. Fruits, sugars, fats, and alcohol do not provide much protein, so a diet based only on these foods would have a good chance of being too low in protein. However, not many vegans we know live on only bananas, hard candy, margarine, and beer. Vegans eating varied diets containing vegetables, beans, grains, nuts, and seeds rarely have any difficulty getting enough protein as long as their diet contains enough energy (calories) to maintain weight. [See the sections on Pregnancy, Lactation, and Infants and Children (pages 176-197) for details about protein needs during these special times.]

What about combining or complementing protein? Doesn't that make the protein issue much more complex? Let's look at a little background on the myth of complementing proteins. Protein is made up of amino acids, often described as its building blocks. We actually have a biological requirement for amino acids, not for protein. Humans cannot make nine of the twenty common amino acids, so these amino acids are considered to be essential. In other words, we must get these amino acids from our diets. We need all nine of these amino acids for our body to make protein.

Some people say that eggs, cow's milk, meat, and fish are high quality protein. This means that they have large amounts of all the essential amino acids. Soybeans, quinoa (a grain), and spinach also are considered high quality protein. Other protein sources of non-animal origin usually have all of the essential amino acids, but the amounts of one or two of these amino acids may be low. For example, grains are lower in lysine (an essential amino acid) and legumes are lower in methionine (another essential amino acid) than those protein sources designated as high quality protein.

Frances Moore Lappe, in her book *Diet for a Small Planet* (6) advocated the combining of a food low in one amino acid with another food containing large amounts of that amino acid. This got to be a very complicated process, with each meal having specific amounts of certain foods in order to be certain of getting a favorable amino acid mix. Many people got discouraged with the complexity of this approach. Actually, Lappe was being overly conservative to avoid criticism from the "Nutrition Establishment." She has since repudiated strict protein combining, saying, "In combating the myth that meat is the only way to get high quality protein, I reinforced another myth. I gave the impression that in order to get enough protein without meat, considerable care was needed in choosing foods. Actually it is much easier than I thought" (7).

Table 3: Amounts of Foods Providing Recommended Amounts of Essential Amino Acids

12-3/4 cups of cooked corn OR 8 large potatoes OR 2-1/2 cups of tofu OR 15-1/2 cups of cooked brown rice

Any one of the above foods, eaten in the amount specified, would provide the recommended amounts of all essential amino acids for an adult male. Women would need about 20% less of each food due to lower recommendations. This concept is illustrated below:

Food	Try	Thr	Iso	Leu	Lys	Met+Cys	Phe+Tyr	Val
Adult RDA, 154 lb male (1)	350	1400	1330	2940	2660	1330	2310	1680
12-3/4 cups corn	437	2527	2527	6801	2679	1824	5339	3629
8 large potatoes	646	2057	2033	2990	3277	1723	3971	3134
2-1/2 cups tofu	780	2045	2480	3808	3298	1333	4112	2530
15-1/2 cups cooked rice	907	2569	2962	5773	2660	2418	6237	4111

Source: USDA Nutrient Database for Standard Reference, Release 24, 2011.

Notes: Amounts of amino acids are in milligrams. Try=tryptophan, Thr=threonine, Iso=isoleucine, Leu=leucine, Lys=lysine, Met+Cys=methionine+cysteine, Phe+Tyr=phenylalanine+tyrosine, Val=valine

We recommend eating a variety of unrefined grains, legumes, seeds, nuts, and vegetables throughout the day, so that if one food is low in a particular essential amino acid, another food will make up this deficit (8,9).

As an extreme example, even if you only ate one kind of grain, bean, potato, or vegetable as a protein source, and ate enough of that food, you could meet your protein and amino acid needs. Admittedly, it would be a very monotonous way to eat and you might miss out on other nutrients. We point this out, however, to illustrate the idea that almost all non-animal protein sources contain all of the essential amino acids. Table 3 (page 145) shows the amount of rice, corn, potatoes, or tofu that an adult male would need to eat if he relied on only one food as a protein source. Women would need about 20% less food because of women's lower protein requirements.

References

1. Food and Nutrition Board, Institute of Medicine. *Dietary Reference Intakes for Energy, Carbohydrate, Fiber, Fat, Fatty Acids, Cholesterol, Protein, and Amino Acids.* Washington, DC: National Academy Press, 2002.

2. Rodriguez NR, DiMarco NM, Langley S. Position of the American Dietetic Association, Dietitians of Canada, and the American College of Sports Medicine: Nutrition and athletic performance. *J Am Diet Assoc* 2009;109:509-27.

3. Mangels R, Messina V, Messina M. *The Dietitian's Guide to Vegetarian Diets, 3rd ed.* Sudbury, MA: Jones and Bartlett Learning, 2011.

4. Sellmeyer DE, Stone KL, Sebastian A, et al. A high ratio of dietary animal to vegetable protein increases the rate of bone loss and the risk of fracture in postmenopausal women. *Am J Clin Nutr* 2001;73:118-22.

5. Knight EL, Stampfer MJ, Hankinson SE, et al. The impact of protein intake on renal function decline in women with normal renal function or mild insufficiency. *Ann Intern Med* 2003;138:460-7.

6. Lappe FM. *Diet for a Small Planet*. New York: Ballantine Books, 1971.

7. Lappe FM. *Diet for a Small Planet*, 10th anniversary edition. New York: Ballantine Books, 1982.

8. Young VR, Pellett PL. Plant proteins in relation to human protein and amino acid nutrition. *Am J Clin Nutr* 1994;59 (suppl):1203S-1212S.

9. Craig WJ, Mangels AR. Position of The American Dietetic Association: Vegetarian Diets. *J Am Diet Assoc* 2009;109:1266-82.

FAT

Summary: Vegan diets are free of cholesterol and generally low in saturated fat. A reasonable goal for most people would be to have no more than 7% (or at most 10%) of calories coming from saturated fat. Total dietary fat should be between 20 and 30% of total calories. Most dietary fat should be in the monounsaturated form from foods like nuts, seeds, olives, avocados, canola oil, and olive oil. Alpha-linolenic acid is an essential omega-3 fat that is found in foods including flaxseed oil, ground flaxseeds, canola oil, and walnuts.

Surveys have shown that vegan adults in the United States eat a slightly lower fat diet than non-vegans do (1). The real difference between vegans and non-vegans, however, is in the types of foods that provide fats. Among the major sources of fat for many adults in the United States are beef, cheese, cow's milk, and poultry (2) — foods that vegans do not eat. Vegans are likely to get their fats from nuts, nut butters, seeds, oils, avocado, olives, coconut, margarine, and soyfoods. These differences explain why vegan diets are often lower in saturated fat, a type of fat that is associated with an increased risk of heart disease.

Experts do not agree about the ideal level of dietary fat and, in fact, there may not be just one ideal level. The Dietary Guidelines for Americans, 2010 call for a total fat intake of 20 to 35% for adults (3). The Food and Agriculture Organization (FAO) of the United Nations recommends that total fats provide from 15% to 35% of calories (4). Significant improvements in symptoms such as angina and reductions in arterial blockage were seen in patients with heart disease who were placed on a near-vegan diet with only 10% of calories from fat (5). While we actually only need 2-3% of calories as fat to insure that we get enough of those fatty acids that our bodies need but cannot produce, a diet with this low of a level of fat would be monotonous and could potentially lead to undesirable weight loss. For most healthy people, a dietary fat level between 20 and 30% of calories seems prudent.

Fat should not be limited for infants less than 1 year. It should be between 30 and 40% of calories for 1 to 3 year olds, and between 25 and 35% of calories for children and teens (3).

Generally, vegan diets can meet fat recommendations if they emphasize grains, legumes, fruits, and vegetables and include moderate amounts of higher fat foods. Including some higher fat foods can help make menus more interesting, provide satiety (a feeling of being comfortably full), and may actually help with weight reduction. Some higher fat foods, like nuts and soy products, can help to reduce the risk of heart disease (6,7). Higher fat foods are also important sources of vitamin E. To provide an idea of what we mean by "moderate amounts," Table 4 shows how much fat would be included in diets of various calorie levels with 20 or 30% of calories from fat. Table 5 shows the amount of fat in common vegetarian foods.

Table 4: Suggested Daily Fat Intake on Different Calorie Levels

1600 calories:
    20% fat   36 grams of fat
    30% fat   53 grams of fat

1800 calories:
    20% fat   40 grams of fat
    30% fat   60 grams of fat

2000 calories:
    20% fat   44 grams of fat
    30% fat   66 grams of fat

2200 calories:
    20% fat   49 grams of fat
    30% fat   73 grams of fat

2400 calories:
    20% fat   53 grams of fat
    30% fat   80 grams of fat

Table 5: Higher Fat Vegan Foods

Food	Fat (grams)
1/4 Avocado	7
1 ounce Dried Shredded Coconut	18
1 ounce Dark Chocolate	9
1/4 cup Coconut Milk	12
1 medium serving French Fries	19
1/2 cup Premium Frozen Vegan Ice Cream (soy- or coconut-based)	5-12
1 Tablespoon Vegan Margarine	9-11
1/4 cup Nuts	16-25
1 Tablespoon Nut or Seed Butter (including peanut butter and tahini)	8-9
1 Tablespoon Oil	13-14
1 ounce Potato Chips	10
1/4 cup Sunflower Seeds	16
1/2 cup Tempeh	9

Table 6: Types of Fat

Saturated fat: a fat that is usually solid at room temperature. Saturated fat raises blood cholesterol more than other forms of fat.

Monounsaturated fat: a fat that is usually liquid at room temperature. This type of fat reduces blood cholesterol when it replaces saturated fat in the diet.

Polyunsaturated fat: a fat that is usually liquid at room temperature. This type of fat also reduces blood cholesterol when it replaces saturated fat in the diet.

Trans fat: when vegetable oils are converted into solid fats, a process called hydrogenation, trans fatty acids are formed. Trans fats may be even worse for the heart than saturated fats.

Type of Fat

Fats are categorized according to their chemical structure as saturated, monounsaturated, polyunsaturated, and trans fats. Saturated fats, found mainly in animal fats and in coconut, palm, and palm kernel oils, are the kind of fats most likely to cause heart disease. They should be limited to no more than 7-10% of calories. Polyunsaturated fats, which are especially high in safflower, sunflower, soybean, and corn oils have long been recommended to replace more saturated fats in order to reduce the risk of heart disease. Recently, much attention has been given to oils high in monounsaturated fats such as olive, peanut, and canola oils. These oils can also replace more saturated fats and apparently reduce the risk of heart disease.

Trans fatty acids are created during food processing when unsaturated oils are changed to be chemically more like solid fats. This process is called hydrogenation and results in *trans* fats which increase risk of heart disease. Intake of these fats should be as low as possible. Since 2006, when companies had to declare the amount of *trans* fats on product labels, the amount of these fats in the food supply in the United States has decreased. Checking labels of margarine, crackers, cookies, and deep-fried foods can let you know if these products contain *trans* fats.

Changing the type of fat you eat may be more important than reducing all fats to very low levels. Replacing fat in the diet with any kind of carbohydrate often lowers the level of HDL cholesterol in the blood. HDL cholesterol is also called "good cholesterol." Replacing saturated fat with polyunsaturated fat and monounsaturated fat can lead to a reduction in LDL (bad) cholesterol (8).

There are two polyunsaturated fatty acids that are essential for humans. These are linoleic acid and linolenic acid. Linoleic acid needs can be easily met by eating a variety of whole foods. Only a limited number of foods provide linolenic acid, an omega-3 fatty acid. These foods include ground flaxseed, flaxseed oil, hempseed oil, canola and walnut oils, walnuts, and full-fat soy products. The Vegan Food Guide found on pages198-199 provides information on the amounts of these foods that should be eaten daily. The linolenic acid found in these foods is used to make EPA and DHA, two other omega-3 fatty acids that seem to play roles in vision and brain development and in heart health. To promote EPA and DHA production, vegans should replace some oils very high in linoleic acid (safflower, sunflower, corn, cottonseed, and soybean oil) with oils that are high in linolenic acid (canola and flaxseed oils) and limit intake of *trans* fatty acids.

What kind of oil should you use? The best choice, based on current knowledge, is one high in monounsaturated fat or in linolenic acid (as described above). Table 7 (page 153) gives the percentage of saturated, monounsaturated, and polyunsaturated fats in various oils and margarines. Whichever you choose, use it with discretion, since oils are high-calorie, high-fat foods.

What about fake fat? Olestra, also called fake fat or Olean, is a fat substitute that has no calories. The U.S. Food and Drug Administration approved it for use in potato chips, tortilla chips, and crackers. Olestra is made from sucrose (sugar) and fatty acids from vegetables. It is not digested or absorbed. Even at low doses (the amount in about 6 potato chips), Olestra significantly reduces blood levels of carotenoids (9). Carotenoids have been repeatedly shown to be important in preventing cancer, heart disease, and eye problems like macular degeneration.

Cholesterol

Vegans do not have to be concerned with dietary cholesterol. Cholesterol is found only in foods of animal origin; so the vegan diet is free of cholesterol. Some plants do contain phytosterols, which have a structure similar to cholesterol. However, phytosterols do not affect blood cholesterol levels. Dietary cholesterol is not necessary since our bodies are able to make all of the cholesterol we need. All of the recipes in this book have no cholesterol.

References

1. Mangels R, Messina V, Messina M. *The Dietitian's Guide to Vegetarian Diets, 3rd ed.* Sudbury, MA: Jones and Bartlett Learning, 2011.

2. Cotton PA, Subar AF, Friday JE, Cook A. Dietary sources of nutrients among US adults, 1994 to 1996. *J Am Diet Assoc* 2004;104:921-30.

3. U.S. Department of Agriculture and U.S. Department of Health and Human Services. *Dietary Guidelines for Americans, 2010.* 7th Edition, Washington, DC: U.S. Government Printing Office, 2010.

4. Food and Agriculture Organization (FAO). *Fats and Fatty Acids in Human Nutrition. Report of an Expert Consultation.* Rome, Italy: FAO, 2010.

5. Ornish D, Schenwitz LW, Billings JH, et al. Intensive lifestyle changes for reversal of coronary heart disease. *JAMA* 1998;280:2001-7.

6. Kris-Etherton PM, Hu FB, Ros E, Sabaté J. The role of tree nuts and peanuts in the prevention of coronary heart disease: multiple potential mechanisms. *J Nutr* 2008;138:1746S-1751S.

7. Zhan S, Ho SC. Meta-analysis of the effects of soy protein containing isoflavones on the lipid profile. *Am J Clin Nutr* 2005;81:397-408.

8. Katan MB, Grundy SM, Willett Wc. Beyond low-fat diets. *N Engl J Med* 1997;337:563-567.

9. Weststrate JA, van het Hof KH. Sucrose polyester and plasma carotenoid concentrations in healthy subjects. *Am J Clin Nutr* 1995; 62:591-597.

Table 7: Typical Fatty Acid Composition of Vegetable Oils and Animal Fats

% of Total Fatty Acids (Notes: Total may not add up to 100% due to rounding. Margarine containing hydrogenated oils is a source of *trans* fatty acids which increase risk of heart disease.)

Oil or Fat	Saturated	Monounsaturated	Polyunsaturated
Coconut oil	92	6	2
Palm kernel oil	86	12	2
Butterfat (not vegan)	68	28	4
Cocoa butter	62	34	3
Palm oil	52	39	10
Beef tallow (not vegan)	52	44	4
Margarine, vegan, stick, non-hydrogenated	43	29	29
Lard (not vegan)	41	47	12
Margarine, vegan, soy, non-hydrogenated	33	33	33
Chicken fat (not vegan)	31	47	22
Margarine, vegan, soy and olive oil, non-hydrogenated	31	31	38
Cottonseed oil	27	19	54
Margarine, vegan, soy-free, non-hydrogenated	25	50	25
Peanut oil	18	49	34
Soybean oil	16	24	60
Olive oil	14	75	11
Corn oil	14	29	57
Sunflower oil (high-oleic)	10	86	4
Safflower oil	8	79	14
Canola oil	7	64	28

Sources: USDA Nutrient Database for Standard Reference, Release 24, 2011 and manufacturers' information.

CALCIUM

Summary: Calcium, needed for strong bones, is found in dark green leafy vegetables, tofu made with calcium sulfate, calcium-fortified soy milk and orange juice, and many other foods commonly eaten by vegans. Although lower animal protein intake may reduce calcium losses, there is currently not enough evidence to suggest that vegans have lower calcium needs. Vegans should eat foods that are high in calcium and/or use a calcium supplement.

Our bones contain large amounts of calcium, which helps to make them firm and rigid. Calcium is also needed for other tasks including nerve and muscle function and blood clotting. These tasks are so important for survival, that, when dietary calcium is too low, calcium will be lost from bone and used for other critical functions. The body tightly controls calcium in the blood, so measuring blood calcium levels cannot assess calcium status.

Because of heavy promotion by the American dairy industry, the public often believes that cow's milk is the sole source of calcium. However, other excellent sources of calcium exist. Sources of well-absorbed calcium for vegans include calcium-fortified soy milk and juice, calcium-set tofu, soybeans and soynuts, bok choy, broccoli, collards, Chinese cabbage, kale, mustard greens, and okra (1). Grains, beans (other than soybeans), fruits, and vegetables (other than those listed) can contribute to calcium intake but cannot replace these key foods. Table 8 (page 156) shows the amount of calcium in selected foods. When you realize that there is as much or more calcium in 4 ounces of firm tofu or 3/4 cup of collard greens as there is in one cup of cow's milk, it is easy to see why groups of people who do not drink cow's milk still have strong bones and teeth.

The calcium recommendation for adults age 19-50 years and men 51-70 years is 1000 mg per day (2). An intake of 1200 mg of calcium is recommended for women over 51 years and for men over 70 (2). While not all studies find a reduced risk of fracturing bones to be associated with higher calcium intakes (3,4), research does suggest that adequate calcium and vitamin D can reduce the risk of fractures and osteoporosis as people age (5).

There are a limited number of studies of vegans, most of which find low bone density, as well as low calcium intakes (6-8). Results of a meta-analysis that combined several studies predicted that vegans would have a slightly (perhaps 10%) higher risk of bone fracture compared to non-vegetarians (8). One study found that, when calcium intakes were adequate (greater than 525 mg/day in this study), vegans had no greater risk of breaking a bone than did non-vegetarians with similar calcium intakes (7). Since many factors can affect calcium needs, we recommend that vegans try to meet the recommendations for the general public.

Our Vegan Food Guide (page 198) indicates good sources of calcium from several food groups. By choosing the suggested number of servings of calcium-rich foods daily, vegans should meet calcium needs. Table 9 (page 157) shows several menus that contain more than 1000 mg of calcium.

The amount of calcium in tofu depends on the coagulating agent used to precipitate the soy protein in the process of making tofu. Calcium sulfate and nigari (magnesium chloride) are two commonly used agents. The agent used will be listed on the label under ingredients. Tofu that is prepared with calcium sulfate will contain more calcium than tofu made with nigari.

To calculate how much calcium is in the tofu you buy, look at the label. Calcium content will be listed as percent of the Daily Value. Since the current Daily Value for calcium is 1000 mg, multiply the percent Daily Value by 10 to get the amount of calcium (in milligrams) in one serving. For example, tofu with 10% Daily Value for calcium would have 100 mg of calcium in one serving.

Protein's effect on calcium needs and bones remains uncertain. Some studies show that diets that are high in protein, especially animal protein, result in increased losses of calcium in the urine (9) and may be associated with increased fracture risk (10,11). These effects of protein may be especially important in those with low calcium intakes (12). Other studies find advantages of a higher protein intake including promotion of calcium absorption (13), reduced risk of fracturing a bone (14), and increased bone density (15,16). Until we know more, our best recommendation is that vegans should strive to meet calcium recommendations and to have adequate, but not excessive, amounts of protein.

Other factors in bone health include vitamin D (see page 169), sodium, and physical activity. Sodium increases the amount of calcium lost in urine (about 20 mg of calcium are lost with each gram of sodium in the diet) and higher dietary sodium is associated with lower bone density (17). Regular weight-bearing exercise such as walking or running helps to promote strong, healthy bones. Exercise can also improve balance and flexibility, important factors in preventing falls.

Table 8: Calcium Content of Selected Vegan Foods

FOOD	AMOUNT	CALCIUM (mg)
Blackstrap molasses	2 Tbsp	400
Collard greens, cooked	1 cup	357
Other plant milks, calcium-fortified	8 ounces	300-500
Tofu, processed with calcium sulfate*	4 ounces	200-420
Calcium-fortified orange juice	8 ounces	350
Soy or ricemilk, commercial, calcium-fortified, plain	8 ounces	200-300
Commercial soy yogurt, plain	6 ounces	300
Turnip greens, cooked	1 cup	249
Tofu, processed with nigari*	4 ounces	130-400
Tempeh	1 cup	184
Kale, cooked	1 cup	179
Soybeans, cooked	1 cup	175
Bok choy, cooked	1 cup	158
Mustard greens, cooked	1 cup	152
Okra, cooked	1 cup	135
Tahini	2 Tbsp	128
Navy beans, cooked	1 cup	126
Almond butter	2 Tbsp	111
Almonds, whole	1/4 cup	94
Broccoli, cooked	1 cup	62

*Read the label on your tofu container to see if it is processed with calcium sulfate or nigari.

Note: Oxalic acid, which is found in spinach, rhubarb, chard, and beet greens binds with the calcium in those foods and reduces its absorption. These foods should not be considered good sources of calcium. Calcium in other green vegetables is well absorbed (1,18). Dietary fiber has little effect on calcium absorption.

Sources: USDA Nutrient Database for Standard Reference, Release 24, 2011 and manufacturers' information.

Table 9: Sample Menus Providing More Than 1,000 Milligrams of Calcium

	Calcium (mg)
Breakfast:	
1 serving Cindy's Light and Fluffy Pancakes (p. 23)	195
1 cup Calcium-Fortified Soy Milk	300
Lunch:	
1 serving Hummus on Pita Bread (p. 27)	178
6 Dried Figs	82
1/4 cup Almonds	94
Dinner:	
1 serving Scrambled Tofu and Bok Choy over Brown Rice (p. 96)	190
1 serving Green Salad and Tangerine Dressing (p. 39)	30
1 serving Chocolate Pudding (p. 114)	92
TOTAL	**1161**

	Calcium (mg)
Breakfast:	
1 serving Tropical Fruit Smoothie (p. 16)	102
1 Toasted medium Bagel with	93
2 Tbsp Almond Butter	111
Lunch:	
1 serving Mini Pizzas (p. 34)	235
1 serving Creamed Spinach (p. 68)	121
Dinner:	
1 serving Lemon Rice Soup (p. 46)	82
1 serving Tofu Squash Burgers (p. 102)	135
1 cup Steamed Broccoli	62
1 serving Chocolate Pudding (p. 114)	92
TOTAL	**1033**

Additional foods should be added to these menus to provide adequate calories and to meet requirements for nutrients besides calcium.

There are factors that increase the risk of osteoporosis and that cannot be changed. These include small frame size, female gender, aging, heredity, being Caucasian or of Asian or Latino descent, early menopause, and prolonged immobilization. Other factors like cigarette smoking, excessive alcohol, physical inactivity, and inadequate calcium and vitamin D (see Chapter on Vitamin D) are under our control. Vegans of all ages can promote bone health by consuming enough calcium and protein, getting adequate vitamin D, limiting use of sodium, and getting regular exercise, especially weight-bearing exercise.

References

1. Weaver CM, Plawecki KL. Dietary calcium: adequacy of a vegetarian diet. *Am J Clin Nutr* 1994;59 (suppl):1238S-1241S.

2. IOM (Institute of Medicine). *Dietary Reference Intakes for Calcium and Vitamin D.* Washington, DC: The National Academies Press, 2011.

3. Feskanich D, Willett WC, Colditz GA. Calcium, vitamin D, milk consumption, and hip fractures: a prospective study among post-menopausal women. *Am J Clin Nutr* 2003;77:504-11.

4. Warensjö E, Byberg L, Melhus H, et al. Dietary calcium intake and risk of fracture and osteoporosis: prospective longitudinal cohort study. *BMJ* 2011 May 24;342.

5. Tang BM, Eslick GD, Nowson C, et al. Use of calcium or calcium in combination with vitamin D supplementation to prevent fractures and bone loss in people aged 50 years and older: a meta-analysis. *Lancet* 2007;370:657-66.

6. Chiu JF, Lan SJ, Yang CY, et al. Long-term vegetarian diet and bone mineral density in post-menopausal Taiwanese women. *Calcif Tissue Int* 1997;60:245-9.

7. Appleby P, Roddam A, Allen N, Key T. Comparative fracture risk in vegetarians and nonvegetarians in EPIC-Oxford. *Eur J Clin Nutr* 2007; 61:1400-6.

8. Ho-Pham LT, Nguyen ND, Nguyen TV. Effect of vegetarian diets on bone mineral density: a Bayesian meta-analysis. *Am J Clin Nutr* 2009; 90:1-8.

9. Kerstetter JE, O'Brien KO, Insogna KL. Low protein intake: the impact on calcium and bone homeostasis in humans. *J Nutr* 2003;133:855S-61S.

10. Frassetto LA, Todd KM, Morris RC, Jr., et al. Worldwide incidence of hip fracture in elderly women: relation to consumption of animal and vegetable foods. *J Gerontol A Biol Sci Med Sci* 2000;55:M585-92.

11. Sellmeyer DE, Stone KL, Sebastian A, et al. A high ratio of dietary animal to vegetable protein increases the rate of bone loss and the risk of fracture in postmenopausal women. *Am J Clin Nutr* 2001;73:118-22.

12. Meyer HE, Pedersen JI, Loken EB, et al. Dietary factors and the incidence of hip fracture in middle-aged Norwegians. A prospective study. *Am J Epidemiol* 1997;145:117-23.

13. Kerstetter JE, O'Brien KO, Caseria DM, et al. The impact of dietary protein on calcium absorption and kinetic measures of bone turnover in women. *J Clin Endocrinol Metab* 2005;90:26-31.

14. Munger RG, Cerhan JR, Chiu BC. Prospective study of dietary protein intake and risk of hip fracture in postmenopausal women. *Am J Clin Nutr* 1999;69:147-52.

15. Kerstetter JE, Looker AC, Insogna KL. Low dietary protein and low bone density. *Calcif Tissue Int* 2000;66:313.

16. Surdykowski AK, Kenny AM, Insogna KL, Kerstetter JE. Optimizing bone health in older adults: the importance of dietary protein. *Aging Health* 2010;6:345-57.

17. Bedford JL, Barr SI. Higher urinary sodium, a proxy for intake, is associated with increased calcium excretion and lower hip bone density in healthy young women with lower calcium intakes. *Nutrients* 2011; 3:951-61.

18. Weaver CM, Heaney RP, Nickel KP, et al. Calcium bioavailability from high oxalate vegetables: Chinese vegetables, sweet potatoes, and rhubarb. *J Food Sci* 1997;62:524-525.

IODINE

Summary: Iodine sources for vegans include iodized salt, iodine supplements, and some sea vegetables. Some sea vegetables can provide too much iodine if used frequently.

Iodine is needed for the thyroid gland to function properly. An iodine deficiency can lead to goiter (enlarged thyroid gland), hypothyroidism, and to impaired mental and physical development in infants and children. In the United States, a major source of iodine is iodized salt. Iodine is also found in seafoods (fish and sea vegetables) and in dairy products. Vegan diets may be low in iodine if they do not include iodized salt or sea vegetables. Studies have reported that iodine intakes of vegans in several countries, including the United States, are lower than those of non-vegetarians (1-3). Low iodine intakes, in conjunction with high intakes of soy products and raw Brussels sprouts, broccoli, cauliflower, and cabbage can result in thyroid problems. Thus, it is prudent for vegans to have regular, reliable sources of iodine.

One simple way to meet iodine needs is by using iodized salt in cooking and at the table. About a half teaspoon of iodized salt provides the recommended amount of iodine (150 micrograms daily for adults (4)). Some brands of sea salt are also iodized — check the label for this information and for the amount of iodine that has been added. For those who prefer to avoid salt, iodine supplements can be used as a source of iodine. Sea vegetables such as kombu or hijiki can serve as alternative iodine sources, but it is easy to get too much iodine from some sea vegetables. As little as 0.6 teaspoon of hijiki or 3-1/3 sheets of nori will meet your daily iodine needs (5). Since too much iodine can also cause health problems, high-iodine sea vegetables should be limited.

Table 10: Iodine Content of Some Sea Vegetables

Sea vegetable	Iodine (micrograms) in a serving	Amount needed to supply 150 micrograms of Iodine (Adult RDA)	Avoid frequent use of more than this amount per day*
Arame	732/Tablespoon	0.6 teaspoon	1.5 Tablespoons
Hiziki	786/Tablespoon	0.6 teaspoon	1.4 Tablespoons
Kombu	1454/1" piece	1/10"	3/4" piece
Nori	40/sheet	3-3/4 sheets	27-1/2 sheets
Wakame	82/Tablespoon	1.8 Tablespoons	0.8 cups

Data from reference 5. All measures are dried (uncooked) sea vegetables. These amounts will vary greatly depending on where the seaweed was gathered and how it was processed and stored.

*Based on Upper Limit of 1100 micrograms of iodine per day. These amounts assume that your diet does not contain other sources of iodine.

References

1. Leung AM, LaMar A, He X, et al. Iodine status and thyroid function of Boston-area vegetarians and vegans. *J Clin Endocrin Metab* 2011; 96:E1303-7.

2. Waldmann A, Koschizke JW, Leitzmann C, Hahn A. Dietary intakes and lifestyle factors of a vegan population in Germany: results from the German Vegan Study. *Eur J Clin Nutr* 2003;57:947-55.

3. Lightowler HJ, Davies GJ. Iodine intake and iodine deficiency in vegans as assessed by the duplicate-portion technique and urinary iodine excretion. *Br J Nutr* 1998;80:529-35.

4. Institute of Medicine, Food and Nutrition Board. *Dietary Reference Intakes for Vitamin A, Vitamin K, Arsenic, Boron, Chromium, Copper, Iodine, Iron, Manganese, Molybdenum, Nickel, Silicon, Vanadium, and Zinc.* Washington, DC: National Academy Press, 2001.

5. Teas J, Pino S, Critchley A, Braverman LE. Variability of iodine content in common commercially available edible seaweeds. *Thyroid.* 2004;14(10):836-841.

IRON

Summary: Dried beans and dark green leafy vegetables are especially good sources of iron, even better on a per calorie basis than meat. Iron absorption is increased markedly by eating foods containing vitamin C along with foods containing iron. Vegetarians do not have a higher incidence of iron deficiency than do meat eaters.

Iron is an essential nutrient because it is a central part of hemoglobin, which carries oxygen in the blood. Iron deficiency anemia is a worldwide health problem that is especially common in young women and in children.

Iron is found in food in two forms, heme and non-heme iron. Heme iron, which makes up 40 percent of the iron in meat, poultry, and fish, is well absorbed. Non-heme iron, 60 percent of the iron in animal tissue and all the iron in plants (fruits, vegetables, grains, nuts) is less well absorbed. Because vegan diets only contain non-heme iron, vegans should be especially aware of foods that are high in iron and techniques that can promote iron absorption. Recommendations for iron for vegetarians (including vegans) may be as much as 1.8 times higher than for non-vegetarians (1).

Some might expect that since the vegan diet contains a form of iron that is not that well absorbed, vegans might be prone to developing iron deficiency anemia. However, surveys of vegans (2,3) have found that iron deficiency anemia is no more common among vegetarians than among the general population although vegans tend to have lower iron stores (3).

The reason for the satisfactory iron status of many vegans may be that commonly eaten foods are high in iron, as Table 11 (page 164) shows. In fact, if the amount of iron in these foods is expressed as milligrams of iron per 100 calories, many foods eaten by vegans are superior to animal-derived foods. This concept is illustrated in Table 12 (page 166). For example, you would have to eat more than 1700 calories of sirloin steak to get the same amount of iron as found in 100 calories of spinach.

Another reason for the satisfactory iron status of vegans is that vegan diets are high in vitamin C. Vitamin C acts to markedly increase absorption of non-heme iron. Adding a vitamin C source to a meal increases non-heme iron absorption up to six-fold which makes the absorption of non-heme iron as good or better than that of heme iron (4).

Fortunately, many vegetables, such as broccoli and bok choy, which are high in iron, are also high in vitamin C so that the iron in these foods is very well absorbed. Commonly eaten combinations, such as beans and tomato sauce or stir-fried tofu and broccoli, also result in generous levels of iron absorption.

It is easy to obtain iron on a vegan diet. Table 13 (page 167) shows several menus whose iron content is markedly higher than the RDA for iron.

Both calcium and tannins (found in tea and coffee) reduce iron absorption. Tea, coffee, and calcium supplements should be used several hours before a meal that is high in iron (5).

References

1. Institute of Medicine, Food and Nutrition Board. *Dietary Reference Intakes for Vitamin A, Vitamin K, Arsenic, Boron, Chromium, Copper, Iodine, Iron, Manganese, Molybdenum, Nickel, Silicon, Vanadium, and Zinc.* Washington, DC: National Academy Press, 2001.

2. Haddad EH, Berk LS, Kettering JD, Hubbard RW, Peters WR. Dietary intake and biochemical, hematologic, and immune status of vegans compared with nonvegetarians. *Am J Clin Nutr* 1999;70(suppl):586S-93S.

3. Obeid R, Geisel J, Schorr H, et al. The impact of vegetarianism on some haematological parameters. *Eur J Haematol.* 2002;69:275-9.

4. Hallberg L. Bioavailability of dietary iron in man. *Ann Rev Nutr* 1981;1:123-147.

5. Gleerup A, Rossander Hulthen L, Gramatkovski E, et al. Iron absorption from the whole diet: comparison of the effect of two different distributions of daily calcium intake. *Am J Clin Nutr* 1995;61:97-104.

Table 11: Iron Content of Selected Vegan Foods

FOOD	AMOUNT	IRON (mg)
Soybeans, cooked	1 cup	8.8
Blackstrap molasses	2 Tbsp	7.2
Lentils, cooked	1 cup	6.6
Spinach, cooked	1 cup	6.4
Tofu	4 ounces	6.4
Bagel, enriched	1 medium	6.4
Chickpeas, cooked	1 cup	4.7
Tempeh	1 cup	4.5
Lima beans, cooked	1 cup	4.5
Black-eyed peas, cooked	1 cup	4.3
Swiss chard, cooked	1 cup	4.0
Kidney beans, cooked	1 cup	3.9
Black beans, cooked	1 cup	3.6
Pinto beans, cooked	1 cup	3.6
Turnip greens, cooked	1 cup	3.2
Potato	1 large	3.2
Prune juice	8 ounces	3.0
Quinoa, cooked	1 cup	2.8
Beet greens, cooked	1 cup	2.7
Tahini	2 Tbsp	2.7
Veggie hot dog, iron-fortified	1 hot dog	2.7
Peas, cooked	1 cup	2.5
Cashews	1/4 cup	2.1
Bok choy, cooked	1 cup	1.8
Bulgur, cooked	1 cup	1.7
Raisins	1/2 cup	1.6
Apricots, dried	15 halves	1.4
Veggie burger, commercial	1 patty	1.4
Watermelon	1/8 medium	1.4
Almonds	1/4 cup	1.3
Kale, cooked	1 cup	1.2
Sunflower seeds	1/4 cup	1.2

(Continued on next page.)

Table 11 continued

FOOD	AMOUNT	IRON (mg)
Broccoli, cooked	1 cup	1.1
Millet, cooked	1 cup	1.1
Soy yogurt	6 ounces	1.1
Tomato juice	8 ounces	1.0
Sesame seeds	2 Tbsp	1.0
Brussels sprouts, cooked	1 cup	0.9

Sources: USDA Nutrient Database for Standard Reference, Release 24, 2011 and Manufacturer's information.

The RDA for iron is 8 mg/day for adult men and for post-menopausal women and 18 mg/day for pre-menopausal women. Vegetarians (including vegans) may need up to 1.8 times more iron.

Table 12: Comparison of Iron Sources

Food	Iron (mg/100 calories)
Spinach, cooked	15.5
Collard greens, cooked	4.5
Lentils, cooked	2.9
Broccoli, cooked	1.9
Chickpeas, cooked	1.8
Sirloin steak, choice, broiled	0.9
Hamburger, lean, broiled	0.8
Chicken, breast roasted, no skin	0.6
Pork chop, pan fried	0.4
Flounder, baked	0.3
Milk, skim	0.1

Note that the top iron sources are vegan.

Table 13: Sample Menus Providing Generous Amounts of Iron

	Iron (mg)
Breakfast:	
1 serving Oatmeal Plus (p. 23)	3.8
Lunch:	
1 serving Tempeh/Rice Pocket Sandwich (p. 94)	4.7
15 Dried Apricots	1.4
Dinner:	
1 serving Black-Eyed Peas and Collards (p. 76)	2.1
1 serving Corn Bread (p. 21)	2.6
1 slice Watermelon	1.4
TOTAL	16.0
Breakfast:	
Cereal with 8 ounces of Soy Milk	1.5
Lunch:	
1 serving Creamy Lentil Soup (p. 49)	6.0
1/4 cup Sunflower Seeds	1.2
1/2 cup Raisins	1.6
Dinner:	
1 serving Spicy Sautéed Tofu with Peas (p. 103)	14.0
1 cup Bulgur	1.7
1 cup Spinach sprinkled with	6.4
2 Tbsp Sesame Seeds	1.2
TOTAL	33.6

Additional foods should be added to these menus to provide adequate calories and to meet requirements for nutrients besides iron.

ZINC

Summary: Zinc sources for vegans include legumes, grains, and nuts.

Zinc is needed for growth, maturation, defense against infections, night vision, taste, and many other functions. The RDA for zinc is 11 milligrams per day for adult men and 8 milligrams per day for adult women (1). Zinc intakes of vegans are generally slightly lower than the RDA and similar to or slightly lower than zinc intakes of non-vegetarians (2-4).

However, besides considering the total amount of zinc we eat, we must also consider what part of that zinc is absorbed and used by our bodies. Phytate, a substance found in whole grains, dried beans, soy products, and nuts, interferes with zinc absorption. Many foods that are high in phytate are also high in zinc (5) so this may partially compensate for the lower zinc absorption from these foods. Some food processing techniques such as leavening bread, fermenting soy products (miso, tempeh), and sprouting beans reduce the effects of phytate and make zinc from these foods more available to our bodies (6).

Vegans should strive for zinc intakes that are higher than the RDA in order to compensate for reduced zinc absorption from many foods that are frequently a part of vegan diets. Good sources of zinc include black-eyed peas, garbanzo beans, lentils, lima beans, green peas, kidney beans, oatmeal, wheat germ, spinach, nuts, tofu, tempeh, textured vegetable protein, and zinc-fortified breakfast cereals and meat analogues.

References

1. Institute of Medicine, Food and Nutrition Board. *Dietary Reference Intakes for Vitamin A, Vitamin K, Arsenic, Boron, Chromium, Copper, Iodine, Iron, Manganese, Molybdenum, Nickel, Silicon, Vanadium, and Zinc.* Washington, DC: National Academy Press, 2001.

2. Haddad EH, Berk LS, Kettering JD, et al. Dietary intake and biochemical, hematologic, and immune status of vegans compared with nonvegetarians. *Am J Clin Nutr* 1999;70(suppl): 586S-93S.

3. Ball MJ, Ackland ML. Zinc intake and status in Australian vegetarians. *Br J Nutr* 2000;83:27-33.

4. Davey GK, Spencer EA, Appleby PN, et al. EPIC-Oxford lifestyle characteristics and nutrient intakes in a cohort of 33883 meat-eaters and 31546 non meat-eaters in the UK. *Public Health Nutr* 2003;6:259-68.

5. Sandstrom B, Arvidsson B, Cederblad A, et al. Zinc absorption from composite meals I. The significance of wheat extraction rate, zinc, calcium, and protein content in meals based on bread. *Am J Clin Nutr* 1980; 33:739-745.

6. Gibson RS, Yeudall F, Drost N, et al. Dietary interventions to prevent zinc deficiency. *Am J Clin Nutr* 1998;68(suppl):484S-487S.

VITAMIN D

Summary: Vitamin D is not found naturally in the vegan diet but can be made by humans following exposure to sunlight. At least 10 to 15 minutes of summer sun on hands and face two or three times a week is recommended for adults so that vitamin D production can occur. Food sources of vitamin D include vitamin D fortified soy milk and rice milk, and mushrooms that have been exposed to ultraviolet light.

Vitamin D is essential for calcium absorption. Failure to obtain enough vitamin D is associated with bone disease in both adults and children. The vegan has no natural, reliable source of vitamin D in the diet. However, this should not be used to argue that we were meant to eat meat. Meat does not contain vitamin D either. In fact, the only significant naturally occurring sources of vitamin D are egg yolks and fatty fish. Mushrooms also contain limited amounts of vitamin D. The vitamin D content of mushrooms can be increased by commercial exposure to ultraviolet light. Vitamin D is added to cow's milk and butter in the USA.

Vitamin D is unique among the vitamins because we can get it in other ways besides through diet. Vitamin D is first activated in the skin upon exposure to sunlight. It goes on to the liver and then to the kidneys where it is converted into the form of vitamin D that regulates bone formation.

Adequate exposure to sunlight, 10 to 15 minutes of summer sun on hands and face two to three times a week, is recommended for adults to obtain adequate vitamin D (1). This recommendation is estimated from studies in infants. Those with darker skin and the elderly (2,3) seem to require longer exposure to sunlight. In the winter months, above latitude 40 degrees N and below 40 degrees S, our skin does not activate vitamin D (4). Sunscreens (5) and air pollution also reduce the amount of vitamin D produced.

Food sources of vitamin D for vegans include some vitamin D fortified breakfast cereals, and vitamin D fortified soy milk and other non-dairy milks. Ergocalciferol, or vitamin D-2, is made on a commercial scale from yeast (6) and is used to fortify some foods. A vegan vitamin D-3 has been recently developed. If you cannot spend time outside routinely and your diet does not include some of these vitamin D sources regularly, a vitamin D supplement is needed. Current recommendations for vitamin D are 15 micrograms (600 IU) for adults 19 through 70 years and 20 micrograms (800 IU) for those 71 and older (7).

References

1. Specker BL, Valanis B, Hertzberg V, et al. Sunshine exposure and serum 25-hydroxyvitamin D concentrations in exclusively breast-fed infants. *J Pediatr* 1985;107:372-376.

2. Clemens TL, Henderson SL, Adams JS, Holick MF. Increased skin pigment reduces capacity of skin to synthesize vitamin D3. *Lancet* 1982;1:74-76.

3. Holick MF. McCollum Award Lecture, 1994: vitamin D: new horizons for the 21st century. *Am J Clin Nutr* 1994;60:619-30.

4. Webb AR, Kline L, Holick MF. Influence of season and latitude on the cutaneous synthesis of vitamin D3: Exposure to winter sunlight in Boston and Edmonton will not promote vitamin D3 synthesis in human skin. *J Clin Endocrinol Metab* 1988;67:373-378.

5. Matsuoka LY, Ide L, Wortsman J, et al. Sunscreen suppresses cutaneous vitamin D synthesis. *J Clin Endocrinol Metab* 1987;64:1165-1168.

6. Bartas J-M. *Vegetarian Journal's Guide to Food Ingredients.* Baltimore, MD: The Vegetarian Resource Group, 1997.

7. IOM (Institute of Medicine). *Dietary Reference Intakes for Calcium and Vitamin D.* Washington, DC: The National Academies Press, 2011.

VITAMIN B12

Summary: The requirement for vitamin B12 is very low, but it is essential. Non-animal sources include Red Star Vegetarian Support Formula or T-6635+ nutritional yeast (a little less than 1 Tablespoon supplies the adult RDA) and vitamin B12 fortified soy milk. It is especially important for pregnant and lactating women, infants, and children to have reliable sources of vitamin B12 in their diets.

Vitamin B12 is needed for cell division and blood formation. Neither plants nor animals make vitamin B12. Bacteria are responsible for producing vitamin B12. Animals get their vitamin B12 from eating foods contaminated with vitamin B12 and then the animal becomes a source of vitamin B12. Plant foods do not contain vitamin B12 except when they are contaminated by microorganisms or have vitamin B12 added to them. Thus, vegans need to look to fortified foods or supplements to get vitamin B12 in their diet. Although recommendations for vitamin B12 are very small, a vitamin B12 deficiency is a very serious problem leading ultimately to irreversible nerve damage. Prudent vegans will include sources of vitamin B12 in their diets. Vitamin B12 is especially important in pregnancy and lactation and for infants and children.

A number of reliable vegan food sources for vitamin B12 are known. One brand of nutritional yeast, Red Star T-6635+, has been tested and shown to contain active vitamin B12. This brand of yeast is often labeled as Vegetarian Support Formula with or without T-6635+ in parentheses following this name. It is a reliable source of vitamin B12. Nutritional yeast, *Saccharomyces cerevisiae*, is a food yeast, grown on a molasses solution, which comes as yellow flakes or powder. It has a cheesy taste. Nutritional yeast is different from brewer's yeast or torula yeast. Those sensitive to other yeasts can often use it.

The RDA for adults for vitamin B12 is 2.4 micrograms daily (1). About 2 rounded teaspoons of large flake Vegetarian Support Formula (Red Star T-6635+) nutritional yeast provides the recommended amount of vitamin B12 for adults (2). A number of the recipes in this book contain nutritional yeast.

Other sources of vitamin B12 are vitamin B12 fortified soy milk, vitamin B12 fortified meat analogues (food made from wheat gluten or soy-beans to resemble meat, poultry, or fish), vitamin B12-fortified energy bars, and vitamin B12 supplements. There are vitamin supplements that do not contain animal products. We recommend checking the label of your favorite product since manufacturers have been known to stop including vitamin B12.

Vegans who choose to use a vitamin B12 supplement, either as a single supplement or in a multivitamin should use supplements regularly. Even though a supplement may contain many times the recommended level of vitamin B12, when vitamin B12 intake is high, not as much appears to be absorbed. This means in order to meet your needs, you should take a daily vitamin B12 supplement of 25-100 micrograms or a twice weekly vitamin B12 supplement of 1000 micrograms (3).

We store between 2 and 5 milligrams of vitamin B12 and only excrete a very small fraction of this each day. Nevertheless, over time, vitamin B12 deficiency can develop if stores are not replenished with vitamin B12 from the diet or from supplements. Although bacteria in the large intes-tine of humans do produce vitamin B12, this vitamin B12 does not appear to be absorbed (4) and is not adequate to prevent a vitamin B12 deficiency (5). Although some vegans may get vitamin B12 from inade-quate hand washing, this is not a reliable vitamin B12 source.

Tempeh, miso, sea vegetables, and other plant foods are sometimes reported to contain vitamin B12. These products, however, are not reli-able sources of the vitamin. The standard method for measuring vitamin B12 in foods measures both active and inactive forms of vitamin B12. The inactive form (also called analogues) actually interferes with normal vitamin B12 absorption and metabolism (6). When only active vitamin B12 is measured, plant foods including fermented soyfoods and sea vegetables do not contain significant amounts of active vitamin B12 (7).

Very small amounts of vitamin B12 have been found in plants grown in soil treated with manure (8). It is not clear whether this vitamin B12 is the active form or the inactive analogue. In any case, the amounts are so small that more than 23 cups of organically grown spinach would have to be eaten every day in order to meet the adult RDA for vitamin B12 (8,9).

References

1. Institute of Medicine, Food and Nutrition Board: *Dietary Reference Intakes for Thiamin, Riboflavin, Niacin, Vitamin B-6, Folate, Vitamin B-12, Pantothenic Acid, Biotin, and Choline.* Washington, DC: National Academy Press, 1998.

2. Lesaffre Yeast Corporation. Vegetarian Support Formula. http://www.lesaffre-yeast.com/red-star/vsf.html. Accessed April 10, 2012.

3. Norris J. Vitamin B12: Are you getting it? http://veganhealth.org/articles/vitaminb12. Accessed April 3, 2012.

4. Armstrong BK. Absorption of vitamin B12 from the human colon. *Am J Clin Nutr* 1968; 21:298-9.

5. Callender ST, Spray GH. Latent pernicious anemia. *Br J Haematol* 1962;8:230-240.

6. Herbert V. Vitamin B12: Plant sources, requirements, and assay. *Am J Clin Nutr* 1988;48:852-858.

7. van den Berg H, Dagnelie PC, van Staveren WA. Vitamin B12 and seaweed. *Lancet* 1988;1:242-3.

8. Mozafar A. Enrichment of some B-vitamin in plants with application of organic fertilizers. *Plant and Soil* 1994;167:305-11.

9. Mozafar A. Is there vitamin B12 in plants or not? A plant nutritionist's view. *Vegetarian Nutrition: An International Journal* 1997;1/2:50-52.

SOURCES OF VITAMINS AND MINERALS

Other vitamins and minerals are generally easy to obtain from a varied diet. Good sources for essential vitamins and minerals are listed below.

Vitamin A - carrots, winter squash, sweet potatoes, pumpkin, collards, spinach, kale, Swiss chard, cantaloupe

Vitamin D - exposure to sunlight, vitamin D-fortified soy milk and other plant milks, vitamin D fortified breakfast cereals

Vitamin E - vegetable oils, soy milk, almond milk, wheat germ, almonds, sunflower seeds, avocado, mango, almond butter

Vitamin K - green leafy vegetables, Brussels sprouts, broccoli

Thiamin - whole grain and enriched breads and cereals, wheat germ, nutritional yeast, legumes, seeds, nuts

Riboflavin - whole grain and enriched breads and cereals, nutritional yeast, wheat germ, soybeans, mushrooms, spinach, almonds, collards

Niacin - whole grain and enriched breads and cereals, peanuts, peanut butter, peas, corn, tempeh, nutritional yeast

Vitamin B6 - soybeans, whole wheat products, lentils, bananas, chick-peas, potatoes, sweet potatoes, spinach

Folacin - spinach, collards, asparagus, legumes, oranges, folic acid-fortified breads and grains, peanuts

Vitamin B12 - Vegetarian Support Formula nutritional yeast (Red Star T6635+), vitamin B12 fortified meat analogues, vitamin B12 fortified breakfast cereals, vitamin B12 fortified soy or other plant milk

(Continued on next page.)

Biotin - lentils, black-eyed peas, almonds, peanut butter

Pantothenic Acid - whole grain cereals, legumes, sunflower seeds

Vitamin C - green and red peppers, cabbage, broccoli, kale, Brussels sprouts, tomatoes, cauliflower, oranges, grapefruit, orange juice, kiwi fruit, cantaloupe, strawberries, pineapple

Calcium - broccoli, kale, collard greens, okra, calcium-precipitated tofu, blackstrap molasses, bok choy, calcium-fortified soy milk and other plant milks, calcium-fortified orange juice, tahini, tempeh

Phosphorus - grains, seeds, dried beans, peas

Iron - green leafy vegetables, dried beans and peas, blackstrap molasses, dried fruits, enriched cereals, soybeans, fortified meat analogues

Magnesium - nuts, legumes, whole grains, spinach, seeds

Zinc - dried beans, corn, oatmeal, brown rice, spinach, seeds, wheat germ, fortified meat analogues, tofu

Copper - soybeans, chickpeas, cashews, chocolate, mushrooms, sunflower seeds, tahini

Iodine - iodized salt, commercial bread, sea vegetables

Selenium - Brazil nuts, pasta, sunflower seeds, brown rice, tofu

Manganese - whole grains and cereals, tea, nuts, legumes, tempeh

Chromium - brewer's yeast, whole grains

Molybdenum - beans, breads, cereals

PREGNANCY AND THE VEGAN DIET

"My doctor says I have to drink a quart of cow's milk a day; my parents are convinced I'm doing something harmful; and I'm even starting to wonder if my diet is all right." Even the most committed and knowledgeable vegan may face doubts when pregnant. After all, the so-called experts are all questioning her dietary choices.

Actually, it is reasonably simple to follow a vegan diet throughout pregnancy while eating foods that meet your needs and the needs of your baby. A series of studies (1,2) at The Farm, a community where vegan diets are a part of a socially responsible lifestyle, have shown that vegans can have healthy pregnancies and healthy children. Here are some things to consider.

Weight Gain

How much weight you gain during your pregnancy has a marked impact on the baby's size and health at birth. Table 14 (page 177) will help you to calculate how much weight you should gain. If you were underweight prior to your pregnancy, you should try to gain 28-40 pounds. Average weight women should aim for a 25-35 pound weight gain, and overweight women should strive to gain 15-25 pounds. Adolescents may need to gain 30-45 pounds. A general trend is to have little weight gain for the first 12 weeks. Then, in the second and third trimesters, a weight gain of a pound a week is common (3).

Many vegans begin pregnancy on the slim side and may gain weight very slowly. If this sounds like you, you will need to eat more food. Perhaps eating more often or eating foods higher in fat and lower in bulk will help. I found it easiest to drink extra calories and treated myself to a soy milk shake (soy milk blended with fruit and tofu or soy yogurt) in the evening for a few weeks when weight gain was low. Other concentrated sources of calories include nuts and nut butters, dried fruits, soy products, and bean dips. Table 15 (page 181) shows some ways of getting some extra calories — you need about 340 extra calories per day in the second and 450 calories per day in the third trimester. If, on the other hand, your weight gain seems too high to you and your health care provider, look at the types of food you are eating. Simply replacing sweets and fatty foods with fruits, vegetables, grains, and legumes can lead to more moderate weight gain. Daily exercise, as approved by your health care provider, can also help.

Table 14: Body Mass Index

Step 1. Take your prepregnant weight (in pounds) and divide it by your height (in inches) squared; then multiply by 700. BMI = lb/in^2 x 700. For example, if I weigh 110 pounds and am 60 inches tall, my BMI is 110/3600 x 700 = 21.4.

Step 2. Use your BMI to find your pre-pregnancy weight-for-height status and the amount of weight you should try to gain in pregnancy.

Pre-pregnancy BMI	Weight-for-height status	Recommended weight gain
<18.5	Underweight	28-40 pounds
18.5 to 24.9	Normal weight	25-35 pounds
25 to 29.9	Overweight	15-25 pounds
>30	Obese	11-20 pounds

Adapted from reference 3.

Protein

You will probably get lots of questions about whether or not you are getting enough protein. Current recommendations for protein in pregnancy call for 25 grams more of protein per day in the second and third trimesters for a total of 71 grams of protein (4). One study showed that the average non-pregnant vegan woman was eating 65 grams of protein daily (5), almost enough to meet the needs during pregnancy. If your diet is varied and contains good protein sources such as soy products, beans, and grains, and you are gaining weight, you can relax and not worry about getting enough protein. Many women simply get the extra protein they need by eating more of the foods they usually eat. As an example, you can add 25 grams of protein to your usual diet by adding 1-1/2 cups of lentils or tofu, 3-1/2 cups of soy milk, or 2 large bagels.

Calcium and Vitamin D

Vegans also get lots of questions about calcium. Both calcium and vitamin D are needed for the development of the baby's bones and teeth. There is some evidence that pregnant women adapt to low calcium intakes and increased needs by increasing calcium absorption and reducing calcium losses (6). This certainly is worthy of additional study and may be pertinent to vegans whose diets may be low in calcium. However, for the time being, calcium intakes of 1300 milligrams daily are recommended for women 18 and younger and of 1000 milligrams daily for women 19 through 50 (7). Pregnant vegans should make a special effort to have 8 or more servings of calcium-rich foods daily. (See the Vegan Meal Plan on page 198 for more details.)

Pregnant women who have regular sunlight exposure do not need any extra vitamin D (7,8). However, if there is any question as to whether or not your sun exposure is adequate, 15 micrograms (600 IU) of dietary and/or supplemental vitamin D (7). Supplements of vitamin D should only be used with the approval of your health care provider since high doses of vitamin D can be toxic. Fortified foods like some brands of soy or other plant milks are another way to meet vitamin D needs.

Iron

Iron deficiency anemia is not uncommon during pregnancy, whether vegan or non-vegetarian. Iron needs are much higher than usual in pregnancy because of the increase in the amount of the mother's blood and because of blood formed for the baby. Iron supplements during the second and third trimester are commonly recommended along with iron-rich foods. Additional iron may be needed in case of iron deficiency. Iron supplements should not be taken with calcium supplements and should be taken between meals in order to maximize absorption. Even when iron supplements are used, pregnant vegans should choose high iron foods like whole grains, dried beans, tofu, and green leafy vegetables daily.

Vitamin B12

The regular use of vitamin B12 supplements or fortified foods is recommended for all pregnant vegans. Vitamin B12 plays an important role in the developing fetus. Fortified foods include some breakfast cereals, some soy milks, and Red Star Vegetarian Support Formula nutritional yeast.

Folate

Folate has been in the news because of its connection with a type of birth defect called neural tube defect. Studies have shown that women who have infants with neural tube defects have lower intakes of folate and lower blood folate levels than other women. Folate is needed early in pregnancy (before many women know they are pregnant) for normal neural tube development. Many vegan foods including enriched bread, pasta, and cold cereal; dried beans; green leafy vegetables; and orange juice are good sources of folate. Vegan diets tend to be high in folate, however, to be on the safe side, women capable of becoming pregnant should take a supplement or use fortified foods that provide 400 micrograms of folate daily.

Docosahexaenoic Acid (DHA)

DHA is a type of fat that is mainly found in fatty fish. It seems to be important in the development of the brain and the retina, a part of the eye. Some DHA can be made from another fat called linolenic acid that is found in flaxseed, flaxseed oil, canola oil, walnuts, and soybeans. Choosing these foods regularly and avoiding foods containing *trans* fats that can interfere with DHA production, can help to enhance DHA production. Some women may opt to use a vegan DHA supplement produced from microalgae.

Iodine

Pregnant vegans who use salt should use iodized salt at the table or in cooking. The American Thyroid Association recommends that pregnant women living in the United States and Canada take a prenatal vitamin containing 150 micrograms of iodine daily (9).

All of this advice to eat a plant-based whole foods diet sounds wonderful to many pregnant women. What are the barriers to eating a healthful vegan diet?

Nausea and vomiting

Nausea and vomiting, also called morning sickness, is a concern of many pregnant women, vegans included. Many women are repulsed by foods that used to make up the bulk of their diet such as salads, dried beans, and soy milk. These aversions are extremely common in early pregnancy and are believed to be due to a heightened sense of smell, possibly due to hormonal changes (10). While every woman and every pregnancy will vary in terms of coping with nausea and vomiting, some things to try appear on page 182.

Table 15: 300 Calorie Snacks

These snacks can help to provide some of the extra calories that are needed in pregnancy. During the second trimester you need about 340 calories more per day and during the third trimester you need about 450 calories daily (compared to your pre-pregnant needs).

1 serving Fruit Whiz (p. 17)
1 serving Pita Chips (p. 36)

2 Apple Raisin Spice Muffins (p. 20)
1/2 cup Soy Milk

1 serving Hummus Spread (p. 27) on
2 slices Whole Wheat Bread

1 serving Cheesy Pita Toast (p. 37)
1 cup Apple Juice

Double serving Tofu Dip (p. 99) with
Fresh Vegetables

3 Ginger Cookies (p. 109)
1 cup Soy Milk

1 serving Karen's Creamy Rice Pudding (p. 115)
1 large Apple

1 cup Soy Yogurt with
2 Tbsp Nuts and Dried Fruit

1 Bagel with
1 Tbsp Almond Butter

1 serving Thick Shake (p. 18)

1 serving Easy Pasta Salad (p. 44)
1 Banana

Double serving Split Pea Dip (p. 36) with
Double serving Pita Chips (p. 36)

1 Mini Pizza (p. 34)

Coping with nausea and vomiting:

- If it tastes good, eat it! I can remember wanting nothing but saltines and ginger ale for days at a time. Then, one day when my husband was warming up some left-over pasta, it smelled wonderful. I ate 3 bowls full and never regretted it.

- Try eating low fat, high carbohydrate foods. These are digested more quickly and stay in the stomach for less time giving less time for queasiness.

- Eat often. Sometimes nausea is really due to hunger.

- Avoid foods that have strong smells. Sometimes cold foods are better tolerated because they don't smell as much. Have someone else do the cooking if possible and go away from the house while cooking is being done.

- Be sure to drink juice, water, soy milk, or miso broth if you can't eat solid food. Keep trying to eat whatever you can.

- Contact your health care provider if you are unable to eat or drink adequate amounts of fluids for 24 hours.

Lack of Time

Whether you're working full time outside the home or at home full time (or some variation), the thought of preparing elaborate meals and snacks will probably seem daunting. Meals do not have to be elaborate. A meal can be as simple as a bowl of cereal and fruit with soy milk, peanut butter and crackers, or a baked potato and a salad. Use convenience foods like canned beans, frozen vegetables, mixes, pre-chopped vegetables, and frozen entrées to reduce preparation time. Use time-saving appliances like crockpots, pressure cookers, and microwave ovens. Plan to have leftovers. Check out some quick and easy vegan cookbooks for ideas.

Your Health Care Provider

While many family practice physicians, obstetricians, and nurse-midwives may be quite knowledgeable about nutrition, many are not familiar with vegetarian and especially vegan diets. Your health care provider may have lots of questions about what you are eating and whether or not you will be able to meet your needs. Look on this as an opportunity to educate someone about vegan nutrition. Try sharing this chapter and other materials from the resource list with your health care provider. Keeping a record of what you eat for several days may help convince your health care provider that what you're doing is fine or may highlight areas needing improvement. If you have specific concerns and questions, you may choose to consult a registered dietitian (RD) with expertise in vegetarian nutrition. Remember, a varied vegan diet can meet your needs and the needs of your baby during this exciting time.

It is also important to think about alcohol and smoking. Moderate to large amounts of alcohol during pregnancy can cause fetal alcohol syndrome, which impairs mental and physical development. Even one or two drinks of alcohol daily are associated with greater risk of health and development problems for the baby. Based on what we know, women should avoid alcohol during pregnancy. Cigarette smoking has been clearly linked to low birth weight, which increases the infant's chance of having a variety of health problems. Smoking should also be avoided during pregnancy.

The Vegan Food Guide on page 198 can be used in pregnancy. Note the modifications to meet increased needs for protein and other nutrients.

Sample Menu Plan for Pregnant Vegans:

BREAKFAST
1/2 cup oatmeal with maple syrup
1 slice whole wheat toast with fruit spread
1 cup EdenSoy Extra soy milk
1/2 cup calcium and vitamin D fortified
   orange juice

SNACK
1/2 whole wheat bagel
   with margarine
Banana

LUNCH
Veggie burger on whole wheat bun with
   mustard and catsup
1 cup steamed collard greens
Medium apple
1 cup EdenSoy Extra soy milk

SNACK
3/4 cup ready-to-eat
   cereal with 1/2 cup
   blueberries
1 cup EdenSoy Extra
   soy milk

DINNER
3/4 cup tofu stir-fried with 1 cup vegetables
1 cup brown rice
Medium orange

SNACK
Whole grain crackers
   with 2 Tbsp peanut
   butter
4 ounces apple juice

Nutritional analysis of sample menu

	RDA/AI
2240 calories	
100 grams protein (18% of calories)	71 grams
55 grams fat (22% of calories)	
336 grams carbohydrate (60% of calories)	
1688 mg calcium	1000 mg
32.5 mg iron	27 mg
11.2 mg zinc	11 mg
2.1 mg thiamin	1.4 mg
1.4 mg riboflavin	1.4 mg
23.1 mg niacin	18 mg
9 mcg vitamin B12	2.6 mcg
4.2 mcg vitamin D	15 mcg (supplement/ sun exposure indicated)
850 mcg folate	600 mcg

References

1. Carter JP, Furman T, Hutcheson HR. Preeclampsia and reproductive performance in a community of vegans. *Southern Med J* 1987;80:692-697.

2. O'Connell JM, Dibley MJ, Sierra J, et al. Growth of vegetarian children: The Farm study. *Pediatrics* 1989;84:475-481.

3. Rasumssen KM, Yaktine AL. *Weight Gain During Pregnancy: Reexamining the Guidelines.* Washington, DC: Institute of Medicine, National Research Council, 2009.

4. Food and Nutrition Board, Institute of Medicine. *Dietary Reference Intakes for Energy, Carbohydrate, Fiber, Fat, Fatty Acids, Cholesterol, Protein, and Amino Acids.* Washington, DC: National Academy Press, 2002.

5. Carlson E, et al. A comparative evaluation of vegan, vegetarian, and omnivore diets. *J Plant Foods* 1985; 6:89-100.

6. Prentice A. Maternal calcium metabolism and bone mineral status. *Am J Clin Nutr* 2000;71(suppl):1312S-16S.

7. IOM (Institute of Medicine). *Dietary Reference Intakes for Calcium and Vitamin D.* Washington, DC: The National Academies Press; 2011.

8. Specker BL. Do North American women need supplemental vitamin D during pregnancy or lactation? *Am J Clin Nutr* 1994;59(suppl):484S-91S.

9. Becker DV, Braverman LE, Delange F, et al. Iodine supplements for pregnancy and lactation — United States and Canada: recommendations of the American Thyroid Association. *Thyroid* 2006;16:949-51.

10. Erick M. Hyperolfaction as a factor in hyperemesis gravidarum. Considerations for nutritional management. *Perspectives in Applied Nutrition* 1994;2:3-9.

LACTATION AND THE VEGAN DIET

The best diet for breast-feeding is very similar to the diet recommended for pregnancy. Protein recommendations are the same, vitamin B12 recommendations are higher, and the recommendations for iron and calories are lower than during pregnancy.

If you eat too little while breast-feeding, you may not produce as much milk. Although the recommended calorie intake is 330 calories above your usual intake for the first six months (1), you still may lose weight because of a loss of calories in breast milk. It is safe to lose about 1/2 to 1 pound a week while breast-feeding but more rigorous dieting is not recommended. As in pregnancy, small frequent meals are the best way to be sure that you are getting enough calories. Since you do need extra fluid while breast-feeding, use nutritious beverages like juices, soy milk, soups, and vegan smoothies to provide calories.

The recommendation for protein is the same as in pregnancy (1) and can be obtained easily from the extra food you are eating. You should still eat good quality food because you are providing all nutrients to your infant. You will need to be careful to get enough vitamin B12, vitamin D, iodine, and DHA in order to be sure that these nutrients are present in your milk in adequate amounts. See the Pregnancy section (pages 176-185) for more information on sources of these nutrients. Requirements for most other nutrients are similar to those in pregnancy and should be obtained from a varied, healthy vegan diet. The Vegan Food Guide (page 198) includes suggestions for food choices for women who are breast-feeding.

Reference

1. Food and Nutrition Board, Institute of Medicine. *Dietary Reference Intakes for Energy, Carbohydrate, Fiber, Fat, Fatty Acids, Cholesterol, Protein, and Amino Acids.* Washington, DC: National Academy Press, 2002.

FEEDING VEGAN KIDS

Many members of The Vegetarian Resource Group are glowing test-imony to the fact that vegan children can be healthy, grow normally, be extremely active, and (we think) smarter than average. Of course it takes time and thought to feed vegan children. (Shouldn't feeding of any child require time and thought?) After all, the years from birth to adoles-cence are the years when eating habits are set, when growth rate is high, and to a large extent, when the sizes of stores of essential nutri-ents such as calcium and iron are determined.

The earliest food for a vegan baby is ideally breast milk. Many benefits to the infant are conveyed by breast-feeding including some enhance-ment of the immune system, protection against infection, and reduced risk of allergies. In addition, breast milk was designed for baby humans and quite probably contains substances needed by growing infants which are not even known to be essential and are not included in infant formulas.

Many books on infant care have sections on techniques and timing of breast-feeding, and we suggest that you refer to one of these for more information. Be forewarned that the books may discourage vegetarian-ism or veganism. They are wrong. With a little attention to detail, vege-tarianism/veganism and breast-feeding are a good combination. In fact, several reports show that milk of vegetarian women is lower in pesti-cides than the milk of women eating typical American diets (1,2).

If you choose to breast-feed, be sure to see the preceding section on lactation to make sure that your milk is adequate for your child. Be especially careful that you are getting enough vitamin B12. If your diet does not contain reliable sources of vitamin B12, your breastfed infants should receive supplements of 0.4-0.5 micrograms of vitamin B12 daily.

See that your infant receives at least 30 minutes of sunlight exposure per week if wearing only a diaper or 2 hours per week fully clothed with-out a hat to maintain normal vitamin D levels (3). Dark-skinned infants require greater sunshine exposure. If sunlight exposure is limited — due to factors like a cloudy climate, winter, or being dark-skinned — infants who are solely breast-fed should receive vitamin D supplements of 10 micrograms (400 IU) per day (4). Vitamin D deficiency leads to rickets (soft, improperly mineralized bones). Human milk contains only very low levels of vitamin D.

The iron content of breast milk is generally low, no matter how good the mother's diet is. The iron which is in breast milk is readily absorbed by the infant, however. The iron in breast milk is adequate for the first 4 to 6 months or longer. Recommendations call for use of iron supplements (1 mg/kg/day) beginning at 4 months to insure adequate iron intake (5). Breast-fed infants may require supplemental fluoride after 6 months if water intake is low and if supplements are prescribed by a dentist or pediatrician.

If for any reason you choose not to breast-feed or if you are using formula to supplement breast-feeding, there are several soy-based formulas available. These products support normal infant growth and development (6). Soy-based formulas are used by vegan families as the best option when breast-feeding is not possible. At this time, all soy for-mulas contain vitamin D derived from lanolin (sheep's wool). Some soy-based formulas (such as Parent's Choice[R] and some store brands) may contain animal-derived fats so check the ingredient label. Soy formulas are used exclusively for the first 6 months.

Soy milk, rice milk, other plant milks, and homemade formulas should not be used to replace breast milk or commercial infant formula during the first year. These foods do not contain the proper ratio of protein, fat, and carbohydrate, nor do they have enough of many vitamins and min-erals to be used as a significant part of the diet in the first year.

Supplemental food (food besides breast milk and formula) can be start-ed at different times in different children depending on the child's rate of growth and stage of development but are usually begun somewhere in the middle of the first year. Some signs of the time to start introducing solid foods are: the ability to sit unsupported, disappearance of the tongue extrusion reflex, increased interest in foods others are eating, and an ability to pick up food and put it in the mouth.

Introduce one new food at a time so that any source of allergies can be later identified. Many people use iron-fortified infant rice cereal as the first food. This is a good choice as it is a good source of iron and rice cereal is least likely to cause an allergic response. Cereal can be mixed with expressed breast milk or soy formula so the consistency is fairly thin. Formula or breast milk feedings should continue as usual. Start with one cereal feeding daily and work up to 2 meals daily or 1/3 to 1/2 cup. Oats, barley, corn, and other grains can be ground in a blender and then cooked until very soft and smooth. These cereals can be introduced one at a time. However, they do not contain much iron, so iron supplements should be continued.

When cereals are well accepted, fruit, fruit juice, and vegetables can be introduced. Fruits and vegetables should be well mashed or puréed. Mashed banana is one food that many infants especially enjoy. Other fruits include mashed avocado, applesauce, and puréed canned peaches or pears. Citrus fruits and juices are common allergens and should not be introduced until the first birthday. Mild vegetables such as potatoes, carrots, peas, sweet potatoes, and green beans should be cooked well and mashed. There is no need to add spices, sugar, or salt to cereals, fruits, and vegetables. Grain foods such as soft, cooked pasta or rice, soft breads, dry cereals, and crackers can be introduced as the baby becomes more adept at chewing. By age 7-8 months, good sources of protein can be introduced. These include well-mashed cooked dried beans, mashed tofu, and soy yogurt. Children should progress from mashed or puréed foods to pieces of soft food. Smooth nut and seed butters can be used to make sauces or dips. To avoid choking, nut and seed butters should not be spread on bread or crackers or given to babies by the spoonful until after the first birthday.

Many parents choose to use commercially prepared baby foods. There are products available for vegan infants. Careful label reading is recommended. Since commercial products contain limited selections for the older vegan infant, many parents opt to prepare their own baby foods. Foods should be well washed, cooked thoroughly, and blended or mashed to appropriate consistency. Home-prepared foods can be kept in the refrigerator for up to 2 days or frozen in small quantities for later use.

By 10-12 months, most children will be eating at least the amounts of foods shown in Table 16 (page 191).

Certainly it makes sense for vegans to continue breast-feeding for a year or longer, if possible, because breast milk is a rich source of nutrients. Vegan infants should be weaned to a fortified soy milk containing calcium, vitamin B12, and vitamin D. Low-fat or non-fat soy milks should not be used before age 2. Milks based on rice, oats, hemp, almonds or other nuts, and coconut are not recommended as a primary beverage for infants and toddlers as they are quite low in protein and energy.

Several studies have been reported showing that the growth of vegan children is slower than that of non-vegans (see 7-9). Studies such as these are often cited as evidence that vegan diets are inherently unhealthy. However, when the studies are examined more closely, we find that they are often based on vegans who have very low calorie or very limited diets (only fruit and nuts for example). In addition, many vegan infants are breastfed. Babies who are breastfed tend to gain weight more slowly before their first birthday than do bottle-fed babies. Up until a few years ago, vegetarians whose babies were breastfed were justly suspicious of growth charts. Before 2006, growth charts for infants were mainly based on the growth of babies fed infant formula. Growth charts based on formula-fed infants may make it seem that breastfed infants are not growing well. In 2006, the World Health Organization (WHO) released growth charts that were based on the growth of breastfed infants (10). These growth charts, which show what normal growth should look like, are called the WHO growth charts and should be used to assess growth of children less than 2 years of age. Older children are monitored with growth charts from the Centers for Disease Control (CDC) (10).

An additional question that must be asked is, "What is a normal growth rate?" Growth rate is assessed by comparing changes in a child's height, weight, and head circumference to rates of growth that have been established by measuring large numbers of apparently healthy children. Once your child's height and weight are measured, the meas-urements are compared to growth curves – graphs that show growth patterns of children by age. There is no single perfect growth rate. Instead, growth charts are set up using percentiles. If your child's height is at the 50th percentile, that means that 50% of children of that age are taller and 50% are shorter. Similarly, a weight at the 25th percentile means 25% of children weigh less and 75% weigh more at the same age.

While some studies show that vegan children are at a lower percentile of weight and height than are other children of a similar age, a recent study shows that vegan children can have growth rates which do not dif-fer from those of omnivorous children of the same age (11). A wide range of growth percentiles are considered "normal." A child at the 10th percentile for weight or the 95th percentile for height is still considered to be within the healthy range. You don't get extra points for higher or lower percentiles. However, if your baby or young child is below the 2nd or above the 98th percentile for weight or head circumference (or below the 2nd percentile for length), your health care provider will try to find out why this is and if intervention is needed. In addition, children don't usually make large jumps – like from the 75th to the 25th percentile – so if this happens, the reason for this faltering is investigated. Older children (age 2 and older) are assessed using slightly different standards. Older children's' body mass index (BMI) is calculated using their weight and height. If BMI for age or weight for height is above the 95th percentile, the child is evaluated as being overweight. If BMI for age is between the 85th and 95th percentile, the child is "at risk of overweight." If BMI for age is below the 5th percentile, the child is considered underweight and further evaluation may be needed (10).

Of course, when any child is evaluated, factors such as the size of the parents and whether or not the child was born prematurely or if there are health issues are taken into consideration.

Table 16: Feeding Schedule For Vegan Babies Ages 6-12 Months

	6 mos	6-8 mos	9-10 mos	11-12 mos
MILK	Breast milk or soy formula.	Breast milk or soy formula.	Breast milk or soy formula.	Breast milk or soy formula (24-32 ounces).
CEREAL & BREAD	Begin iron-fortified baby cereal mixed with milk.	Continue baby cereal. Begin other breads and cereals.	Baby cereal. Other breads and cereals.	Baby cereal until 18 mos. Total of 4 servings (1 serving=1/4 slice bread or 2-4 Tbsp cereal).
FRUITS & VEGETABLES	None	Begin juice from cup: 2-4 ounces vit C source. Begin mashed vegetables & fruits.	4 oz. juice. Pieces of soft/cooked fruits and vegetables.	Table-food diet. Allow 4 servings per day (1 serving= 2-4 Tbsp fruit & vegetable, 4 oz. juice).
LEGUMES & NUT BUTTERS	None	Gradually introduce tofu, puréed legumes, & soy yogurt	Tofu, casseroles, puréed legumes, soy cheese, & soy yogurt.	2 servings daily each about 1/2 oz.

The best way to assure that your children achieve their ideal rate of growth is to make sure that they have adequate calories. Some vegan children have difficulty getting enough calories because of the sheer bulk of their diets. Children have small stomachs and can become full before they have eaten enough food to sustain growth. The judicious use of fats in forms like avocados, nuts, nut butters, seeds, and seed butters will provide a concentrated source of calories needed by many vegan children. Dried fruits are also a concentrated calorie source and are an attractive food for many children. Teeth should be brushed after eating dried fruits to prevent tooth decay.

Are very low fat diets appropriate for children? Some parents wish to reduce their children's risk of developing heart disease later in life and markedly restrict the fat in their children's diets (10 to 15 percent of calories from fat). In some cases, a very low fat diet can compromise a child's growth because the child is not getting enough calories. There is no evidence that a very low fat diet is any healthier for a vegan child than a diet that has somewhat more fat (25 to 35 percent of calories from fat). Fat should not be limited for infants less than 2 years. It should be between 30 and 40% of calories for 1 to 3 year olds, and between 25 and 35% of calories for 2 to 3 year olds, and between 25 and 35% of calories for children and teens (12). If you are using a lower fat diet than this, check that the child's growth is normal and that the child is eating enough food to meet nutrient needs.

Diets of young children should not be overly high in fiber since this may limit the amount of food they can eat. The fiber content of a vegan child's diet can be reduced by giving the child some refined grain products, fruit juices, and peeled vegetables.

Sources of protein for vegan children include legumes, grains, tofu, tempeh, soy milk, nuts, peanut butter, tahini, soy hot dogs, soy yogurt, and veggie burgers. Some of these foods should be used daily. Children should get enough calories so that protein can be used for growth in addition to meeting energy needs.

Table 17 (page 193) shows one diet plan that has been used success-fully by vegan children (adapted from 13).

Table 17: Diet Plans For Vegan Children

TODDLERS AND PRESCHOOLERS, 1-3 YEARS

FOOD GROUP	NUMBER OF SERVINGS
GRAINS	6 or more (a serving is 1/2 to 1 slice of bread or 1/4 to 1/2 cup cooked cereal or grain or pasta or 1/2 to 1 cup ready-to-eat cereal)
LEGUMES, NUTS, SEEDS	2 or more (a serving is 1/4 to 1/2 cup cooked beans, tofu, tempeh or TVP; or 1 ounce of meat analogue; or 1 to 2 Tbsp nuts, seeds, or nut butters or seed butters. Include at least 1 serving of nuts, seeds, or a full-fat soy product.
FORTIFIED SOY MILK, ETC.	3 (a serving is 1 cup fortified soy milk, infant formula, or breast milk)
VEGETABLES	2 or more (a serving is 1/4 to 1/2 cup cooked or 1/2 to 1 cup raw vegetables)
FRUITS	3 or more (a serving is 1/4 to 1/2 cup canned fruit or 1/2 cup juice, or 1 medium fruit)
FATS	3-4 (1 tsp. margarine or oil) (use ½ tsp. flaxseed oil or 2 tsp. canola oil daily to supply omega-3 fatty acids)

CHILDREN, 4-13 YEARS

(Note: See the Vegan Food Guide on Page 198 for information on serving sizes and the starred food items.)

FOOD GROUP	NUMBER OF SERVINGS
GRAINS	8 or more for 4 to 8 yr olds; 10 or more for 9 to 13 yr olds
PROTEIN FOODS	5 or more for 4 to 8 yr olds; 6 or more for 9 to 13 yr olds
VEGETABLES	4 or more
FRUITS	2 or more
FATS	2 or more for 4 to 8 yr olds; 3 or more for 9 to 13 yr olds
OMEGA-3 FATS	1 per day
STARRED FOOD ITEMS	6 or more for 4 to 8 yr olds; 10 or more for 9 to 13 yr olds

Adapted from (13). See Notes on next page.

Notes: Serving sizes vary depending on the child's age.

The calorie content of the diet can be increased by greater amounts of nut butters, dried fruits, soy products, and other high calorie foods.

A regular source of vitamin B12 like Vegetarian Support Formula nutritional yeast, vitamin B12 fortified soy milk, vitamin B12 fortified breakfast cereal, vitamin B12 fortifed meat analogues, or vitamin B12 supplements should be used.

Adequate exposure to sunlight, 20 to 30 minutes of summer sun on hands and face two to three times a week, is recommended to promote vitamin D synthesis (3,4). If sunlight exposure is limited, dietary or supplemental vitamin D should be used.

Although today more and more children are vegan from birth, many older children also become vegan. There are many ways to make a transition from a non-vegan to a vegan diet. Some families gradually eliminate dairy products and eggs, while others make a more abrupt transition. Regardless of which approach you choose, be sure to explain to your child what is going on and why, at your child's level. Offer foods that look familiar, at first. Peanut butter sandwiches seem to be universally popular (beware: some kids are allergic to peanut butter) and many children like pasta or tacos. Gradually introduce new foods. Watch your child's weight closely. If weight loss occurs or the child doesn't seem to be growing as rapidly, add more concentrated calories and reduce the fiber in your child's diet.

Teenage Vegans

Teenage vegans have nutritional needs that are the same as any other teenager. The years between 13 and 19 are times of especially rapid growth and change. Nutritional needs are high during these years. The teenage vegan should follow the same recommendations that are made for all vegans, namely to eat a wide variety of foods, including fruits, vegetables, plenty of leafy greens, whole grain products, nuts, seeds, and legumes. The nutrients teenage vegans should be aware of are protein, calcium, iron, and vitamin B12.

The recommendation for protein is 0.43 grams per pound of weight for 11-13 year olds and 0.4 grams per pound of weight for 14-18 year olds

(12). Those exercising strenuously (marathon runners, for example) may need slightly more protein. A 16 year old who weighs 120 pounds, needs about 48 grams of protein daily. In terms of food, 1 cup of cooked dried beans has about 15 grams of protein, a cup of soy milk has 7 grams, 4 ounces of tofu has 10-11 grams, a Tablespoon of peanut butter or peanuts has 4 grams, and 1 slice of bread or 1 cup of grain has about 3 grams.

Fruits, fats, and alcohol do not provide much protein, and so a diet based only on these foods would have a good chance of being too low in protein. Vegans eating varied diets containing vegetables, beans, grains, nuts, and seeds rarely have any difficulty getting enough protein as long as their diet contains enough energy (calories) to support growth. There is no need to take protein supplements. There is no health benefit to eating a very high protein diet and it will not help in muscle building.

During adolescence, calcium is used to build bones. The density of bones is determined in adolescence and young adulthood, and so it is important to include good sources of calcium in a teen-ager's diet every day.

Cow's milk and dairy products do contain calcium. However, there are other good sources of calcium such as tofu processed with calcium sulfate, green leafy vegetables including collard greens, mustard greens, and kale, as well as tahini (sesame butter), fortified soy milk, and fortified orange juice.

By eating a varied diet, a vegan can meet his or her iron needs, while avoiding the excess fat and cholesterol found in red meats such as beef or pork. To increase the amount of iron absorbed from a meal, eat a food containing vitamin C as part of the meal. Citrus fruits and juices, tomatoes, and broccoli are all good sources of vitamin C. Foods that are high in iron include broccoli, watermelon, spinach, black-eyed peas, blackstrap molasses, chickpeas, and pinto beans.

It is important to consume adequate vitamin B12 during adolescence. Vitamin B12 is not found in plants. Some cereals have vitamin B12 (check the label). Red Star Vegetarian Support Formula nutritional yeast supplies vitamin B12.

Many teenagers are concerned with losing or gaining weight. To lose weight, look at the diet. If it has lots of sweet or fatty foods, replace them with fruits, vegetables, whole grains, and legumes. If a diet already seems healthy, increased exercise — walking, running, or swimming daily — can help control weight. To gain weight, more calories are needed. Perhaps eating more often or eating foods somewhat higher in fat and lower in bulk will help. Try to eat three or more times a day whether you are trying to gain weight or lose weight. It is hard to get all of the nutritious foods you need if you only eat one meal a day. If you feel that you cannot control your eating behavior or if you are losing a great deal of weight, you should discuss this with your health care provider.

Often there is just not enough time to eat. Below are some foods that kids can eat as snacks on the run. Some of these foods can be found in fast-food restaurants — check the menu. Ideas for snacks that you can carry from home include: apples, oranges, bananas, grapes, peaches, plums, dried fruits, bagels and peanut butter, carrot or celery sticks, popcorn, pretzels, soy cheese pizza, bean tacos or burritos, salad, soy yogurt, soy milk, rice cakes, sandwiches, frozen juice bars.

References

1. Dagnelie PC, van Staveren WA, Roos AH, et al. Nutrients and contaminants in human milk from mothers on macrobiotic and omnivorous diets. *Eur J Clin Nutr* 1992;46:355-366.

2. Hergenrather J, Hlady G, Wallace B, et al. Pollutants in breast milk of vegetarians. *N Engl J Med* 1981;304:792 (letter).

3. Specker BL, Valanis B, Hertzberg V, et al. Sunshine exposure and serum 25-hydroxyvitamin D concentrations in exclusively breast-fed infants. *J Pediatrics* 1985;107:372-376.

4. Wagner CL, Greer FR; American Academy of Pediatrics Section on Breastfeeding; American Academy of Pediatrics Committee on Nutrition. Prevention of rickets and vitamin D deficiency in infants, children, and adolescents. *Pediatrics.* 2008;122:1142–52.

5. Baker RD, Greer FR, the Committee on Nutrition. Diagnosis and prevention of iron deficiency and iron-deficiency anemia in infants and young children (0-3 years of age). *Pediatrics* 2010;126:1040-1050.

6. Committee on Nutrition, American Academy of Pediatrics. Soy protein-based formulas: Recommendations for use in infant feeding. *Pediatrics* 1998;101:148-153.

7. Fulton JR, Hutton CW, Stitt KR. Preschool vegetarian children. *J Am Diet Assoc* 1980;76:360-365.

8. Sanders TAB, Purves R. An anthropometric and dietary assessment of the nutritional status of vegan pre-school children. *J Hum Nutr* 1981; 35:349-357.

9. Shinwell ED, Gorodischer R. Totally vegetarian diets and infant nutrition. *Pediatrics* 1982;70: 582-586.

10. Centers for Disease Control. Growth Charts. http://www.cdc.gov/growthcharts/. Accessed April 12, 2012.

11. O'Connell JM, Dibley MJ, Sierra J, et al: Growth of vegetarian children: The Farm study. *Pediatrics* 1989;84:475-481.

12. Food and Nutrition Board, Institute of Medicine. *Dietary Reference Intakes for Energy, Carbohydrate, Fiber, Fat, Fatty Acids, Cholesterol, Protein, and Amino Acids.* Washington, DC: National Academy Press, 2002.

13. Mangels R, Messina V, Messina M. *The Dietitian's Guide to Vegetarian Diets,* 3rd ed. Sudbury, MA: Jones and Bartlett Learning, 2011.

Table 18: Vegan Food Guide

Like any food plan, this should only serve as a general guide for adults. The plan can be modified according to your own personal needs. Individuals with special health needs should consult a registered dietitian or a medical doctor knowledgeable about vegetarian nutrition.

A. PROTEIN FOODS: 5-6 SERVINGS PER DAY (7 FOR PREGNANT WOMEN, 8 FOR WOMEN WHO ARE BREAST-FEEDING)
Note: Each of the following equals one serving.
- 1/2 cup cooked dried beans or peas
- 1/2 cup soybeans*
- 1/2 cup calcium-set tofu** (count as 2 starred food items)
- 1/2 cup tempeh*
- 1 cup calcium-fortified soy milk** (count as 2 starred food items)
- 1/4 cup almonds*, cashews, walnuts, pecans, or peanuts
- 2 Tablespoons peanut butter, tahini*, or almond butter*
- 1 ounce meat analog (burger, dog, deli slices, etc.)
- 1/4 cup soynuts
- 1 cup calcium-fortified soy yogurt** (count as 2 starred food items)

B. WHOLE GRAINS: at least 6-8 SERVINGS PER DAY
Note: Each of the following equals one serving.
- 1 slice whole wheat, rye, or other whole grain bread
- 1/2 whole grain bagel or English muffin
- 1 buckwheat or whole wheat pancake or waffle
- 1 two-inch piece cornbread
- 1 whole grain muffin or biscuit or whole grain tortilla
- 2 Tablespoons wheat germ
- 1 ounce wheat or oat bran
- 1/4 cup sunflower, sesame, or pumpkin seeds
- 3/4 cup wheat, bran, or corn flakes
- 1/2 cup cooked oatmeal or farina
- 1/2 cup cooked brown rice, barley, bulgur, or corn
- 1/2 cup cooked whole wheat noodles, macaroni, or spaghetti

C. VEGETABLES: at least 2-3 SERVINGS PER DAY
1. At least one serving per day of any of the following: 1 cup cooked or 2 cups raw broccoli*, bok choy*, Brussels sprouts, collards*, kale*, mustard greens*, chard, spinach, romaine lettuce, carrots, sweet potatoes, winter squash, or tomatoes.

2. At least one serving per day (one serving equals 1 cup cooked or 2 cups raw) of any other vegetable.

Table 18 continued

D. FRUITS: 2-6 SERVINGS PER DAY

    1. At least 2 servings per day of any of the following: 3/4 cup berries, 1/4 cantaloupe, 1 orange, 1/2 grapefruit, 1 lemon or lime, 1/2 papaya, 4-inch x 8-inch watermelon slice; or 1/2 cup orange, grapefruit, calcium-fortified**, or vitamin C enriched juice.

    2. Additional servings as desired of other fruits: 1 small piece fresh fruit, 3/4 cup grapes, 1/2 cup cooked fruit or canned fruit without sugar, or 2 Tablespoons raisins, dates, or dried fruit.

E. FATS: 0-4 SERVINGS PER DAY

Note: Each of the following equals one serving.

1 teaspoon vegan soft margarine or oil, 2 teaspoons vegan mayonnaise or salad dressing, 1 Tablespoon soy cream cheese or gravy

F. OMEGA-3 FATS: 3 SERVINGS PER DAY FOR MEN; 2 SERVINGS PER DAY FOR WOMEN

Note: Each of the following equals one serving.

1/4 teaspoon flaxseed oil, 1 teaspoon canola or walnut oil, 2/3 teaspoon hempseed oil, 1 teaspoon ground flaxseed, 2 teaspoons chopped walnuts, 1 Tablespoon peanut butter with flaxseed oil.

G. STARRED (*) FOOD ITEMS INDICATE CALCIUM-RICH FOODS: 8 OR MORE SERVINGS PER DAY; 10 OR MORE SERVINGS FOR THOSE AGE 51 AND OLDER

Note: Also counts as servings from other groups.

H. VITAMIN B12 SOURCES: 2 SERVINGS PER DAY; 3 FOR PREGNANT OR BREAST-FEEDING WOMEN

Note: Each of the following equals one serving.

1 Tablespoon Red Star Vegetarian Support Formula nutritional yeast, 1 cup fortified soy milk, 1 ounce fortified breakfast cereal, 1-1/2 ounces fortified meat analogs. If these foods are not eaten regularly, a vitamin B12 supplement (25-100 micrograms daily or 1000 micrograms twice weekly) should be used.

I. ADDITIONAL COMMENTS

    1. Additional servings from one or more food groups may be needed to meet energy needs especially for pregnant and breast-feeding women and physically active people.

    2. This meal plan is for vegan adults. Meal plans for children can be found on page 193.

NUTRITION GLOSSARY

Absorption - taking up nutrients into the blood from the stomach and small and large intestines. Nutrients must be absorbed in order to be used by the body.

Adequate - providing all of the essential nutrients, fiber, and energy in amounts which are enough to meet needs.

Amino acids - building blocks of protein. There are nine amino acids which the human body cannot make in amounts high enough to meet needs. These are called essential amino acids and must be present in one's diet.

Anemia, iron deficiency - reduction in the size of red blood cells due to iron deficiency. Smaller red blood cells are less able to carry oxygen to meet the needs of the body.

Availability - how well a nutrient can be absorbed.

Calorie - a measure of the amount of energy provided by a food. A chemist would define a calorie as the amount of heat needed to raise the temperature of a liter of water 1 degree Celsius.

Carbohydrate - a compound which is made of simple sugars or groups of simple sugars. Carbohydrates are often called sugars and starches.

Carbohydrate, complex - starches or fiber. There are 2 basic types of carbohydrates: complex and simple. Simple carbohydrates are also called sugars.

Cholesterol, blood - the amount of cholesterol found in the blood. High blood cholesterol levels are associated with greater risk for heart disease. Blood cholesterol levels below 200 milligrams per 100 milliliters of blood are recommended by the American Heart Association and other public health groups to reduce the risk of developing heart disease.

Cholesterol, dietary - the amount of cholesterol which occurs in the diet. Cholesterol is a waxy substance, found only in foods of animal origin. Diets which are high in cholesterol have been associated with increased risk of heart disease. It is not necessary to have any cholesterol in the diet because the human body makes all the cholesterol it needs.

Daily Value - a term that appears on food labels. It is used to compare the amount of fat, fiber, vitamins, minerals, and other nutrients in a food to the amounts which should be consumed each day. Daily Values for fat, saturated fat, total carbohydrate, and fiber are based on a 2000 calorie diet. Your Daily Values may be lower or higher depending on your calorie needs. Some Daily Values are maximums (fat, for example, less than 65 grams). If you want to eat less fat than the government recommends (30% of calories), you would want to eat less than 65 grams daily. See Table 19 (page 204) for Daily Values.

Diet - a style or way of eating.

Dietary fiber - the fiber in foods which resists human digestion.

Dietitian - often used as a shortened name for a registered dietitian (see definition). However, in many states the title "dietitian" is not legally protected and can be used by anyone.

Digestion - the physical and chemical breaking down of food to a form which can be used by the body.

Essential - description of a nutrient which cannot be produced by the body in amounts high enough to meet needs and therefore must be ingested in the diet.

Fat - an oily or greasy material which is found in animal tissue and plant seeds. The term fat is often used to mean both fats and oils. Lipid is another term which is used for fat.

Fiber - the part of food which is not digested by humans. (See also dietary fiber.)

Food and Nutrition Board - a section of the National Academy of Sciences which oversees the production of the Recommended Dietary Allowances.

Gram - a unit for measuring weight. A gram is the weight of 1 cubic centimeter or 1 milliliter of water under defined conditions of temperature and pressure. Commonly abbreviated gm.

HDL (high density lipoprotein) cholesterol - often called "good cholesterol." HDL cholesterol is measured as part of a blood lipid profile. Higher levels of HDL appear to reduce the risk of heart disease.

Hydrogenated fat - an unsaturated fat which has had hydrogen added to it in processing to make it more solid and more like a saturated fat. Many margarines and other processed foods contain hydrogenated or partially hydrogenated fats.

LDL (low density lipoprotein) cholesterol - often called "bad cholesterol." LDL cholesterol is measured as a part of a blood lipid profile. Higher levels of LDL appear to increase the risk of heart disease. The level of LDL cholesterol can often be reduced by reducing the amount of saturated fat and cholesterol in one's diet.

Microgram - 1/1,000,000 of a gram. Commonly abbreviated mcg.

Milligram - 1/1,000 of a gram. Commonly abbreviated mg.

Mineral - a naturally occurring inorganic substance. Some essential minerals include calcium, iron, sodium, and zinc.

Monounsaturated fat - canola, olive, and peanut oils are all high in monounsaturated fats. A monounsaturated fat has a chemical structure which includes one double bond.

National Academy of Sciences - a private non-profit group which advises the United States government on science and health issues.

Nutrient - a component of food that helps to nourish the body. Nutrients are classified as protein, fats, carbohydrates, vitamins, minerals, and water.

Nutrition - the science that interprets the relationship of food and diet to the function and health of a living being.

Nutritionist - in some states, by legal definition, refers to an individual with advanced degrees (masters or Ph.D.) in nutrition or a related field from an accredited institution. In other states, this term is not regulated and can be used by anyone.

Obesity - excessive body fatness. Obesity is most often determined by calculating body mass index (BMI) (weight/height^2) and comparing this to standards.

Osteoporosis - a condition in which bones become porous and brittle.

Overweight - weight which is above the recommended weight for a specific height but is less than what is defined as obese.

Polyunsaturated fat - fat which is usually liquid at room temperature. Safflower, sunflower, corn, and soybean oils are all high in polyunsaturated fat. Polyunsaturated fats have a chemical structure which includes more than one double bond.

Protein - a nutrient which contains nitrogen and is made up of amino acids.

Recommended Dietary Allowance (RDA) - the level of intake of an essential nutrient, that, on the basis of scientific knowledge, is judged by the Food and Nutrition Board of the National Academy of Sciences to be adequate to meet the known needs of practically all healthy persons.

Registered Dietitian (R.D.) - an individual who has a degree in nutrition and food sciences from an accredited institution, has completed a year or more of clinical internship or other approved experience, and has passed a national examination. R.D.'s are also required to maintain up-to-date knowledge of nutrition through continuing education.

Requirement - the amount of a nutrient which will just prevent the development of deficiency symptoms. Requirements are different from recommendations since recommendations usually are more generous.

Saturated fat - a fat which is usually solid at room temperature. Coconut and palm oils and animal fats are especially high in saturated fat. Saturated fat has a chemical structure which includes no double bonds.

Varied diet - a diet which includes different foods, the opposite of a monotonous diet.

Vegan - a vegetarian who does not use any animal products such as eggs, dairy products, honey, wool, and leather, etc.

Vegetarian - a person who chooses to abstain from meat, fish, and poultry.

Vitamin - a compound which is essential for life and is needed in very small amounts.

Table 19: Daily Values

Protein (for adults and children 4 or more years of age)	50 gm
Fat	Less than 65 gm
Saturated Fat	Less than 20 gm
Cholesterol	Less than 300 mg
Total Carbohydrate	300 gm
Fiber	25 gm
Sodium	Less than 2400 mg
Potassium	3500 mg
Vitamin A	5000 IU
Vitamin C	60 mg
Thiamin	1.5 mg
Riboflavin	1.7 mg
Niacin	20 mg
Calcium	1000 mg
Iron	18 mg
Vitamin D	400 IU
Vitamin E	30 IU
Vitamin B6	2 mg
Folate	400 mcg
Vitamin B12	6 mcg
Phosphorus	1000 mg
Iodine	150 mcg
Magnesium	400 mg
Zinc	15 mg
Copper	2 mg
Biotin	300 mcg
Pantothenic acid	10 mg

CRUELTY-FREE SHOPPING

Note: The following pages contain the names of companies and organizations offering cruelty-free products, including vegan food, cosmetics and household products that have not been tested on animals and are environmentally sound, as well as clothes and accessories not made with animal products. In addition, this section lists places to buy educational materials on these topics and a bibliography.

When this book was first conceived, few mail-order companies sold vegan items. Now, there are many cruelty-free mail-order companies and online shops. We hope that readers of *Simply Vegan* will support these companies and tell them that they first heard about them in this book. Please let us know if any of these companies change their address or go out of business. In addition, because this book will be updated from time to time, please send us the names and addresses of any other cruelty-free mail-order companies that are not listed here.

VEGAN FOOD THROUGH THE MAIL

Condiments
Annie's Naturals, 1610 Fifth Street, Berkeley, CA 94710, offers organic Smoky Maple BBQ Sauce, (vegan) Worcestershire Sauce, Ketchup, and Mustard. Call (800) 288-1089 or visit <www.annies.com>.

Cultures
Those who live in urban areas usually do not have trouble buying tofu or tempeh. However, for those who cannot locate soy products in their area or city dwellers who would like to try making their own tempeh and other soy products, the following companies should be of help. **The Tempeh Lab Inc.**, sells *Rhizopus oligosporus* culture for making tempeh commercially and at home. Call (931) 964-3574. **G.E.M. Cultures**, P.O. Box 39426, Lakewood, WA 98496, offers a tempeh starter, miso, amazake, shoyu, tamari starters, coagulants for curdling tofu, and a fresh sourdough culture. Visit <www.gemcultures.com> or call (253) 588-2922.

Dried Foods for Backpacking and Cycling

Crunchies Food Company, 790 Hampshire Road, Suite H, Westlake Village, CA 91361 offers freeze-dried fruit and veggies. Call (888) 997-1866 or visit <www.crunchiesfood.com>; **Mary Jane Farm Back Country Foods**, P.O. Box 8691, Moscow, ID 83843, offers a wide variety of organic backpacking foods of which many are vegan. Call (888) 750-6004 or visit <www.backcountryfood.org>; **Nile Spice Foods, Inc.**, Hain Celestial Group, Inc., 4600 Sleepytime Dr. Boulder, CO 80301, manufactures light-weight meals in a cup. Call (800) 434-4246 or visit <www.nilespice.com>; and **Wilderness Dining** offers several vegan meals. Call (866) 576-0642 or visit <www.wildernessdining.com>.

Fruits and Vegetables

Brooks Tropicals, P.O. Box 900160, Homestead, FL 33090 offers tropical fruits and vegetables, including items that are often difficult to locate. Visit <www.brookstropicals.com>; **Door to Door Organics**, offers delivery of organic produce. Visit <www. doortodoororganics.com>; and **World Variety Produce, Inc.**, P.O. Box 514599, Los Angeles, CA 90051 offers Melissa's Specialty Foods including fruit baskets and dried fruit. Call (800) 588-0151 or visit <www.melissas.com>.

Natural Foods Products Mail-Order/Online Companies

More and more companies offer natural foods products through the mail and online. This is a partial list. **Frankferd Farms**, 717 Saxonburg Blvd., Saxonburg, PA 16056. Call (724) 352-9500 or visit <www.frankferd. com>; **Gold Mine Natural Food Company**, 7805 Arjons Drive, San Diego, CA 92126. Call (800) 475-3663 or visit <www.shop.goldmine naturalfoods.com>. Offers organic foods, books, and household products; **Jaffe Brothers Natural Foods**, 28560 Lisac Road, Valley Center, CA 92082. Visit <www.organicfruits andnuts.com> or call (877) 975-2333; **Lumen Foods**, 409 Scott Street, Lake Charles, LA 70601. Call (337) 436-6748 or visit <www.soybean. com>. Offers a variety of meatless meat items plus more; **Mail Order Catalog**, 413 Farm Road, P.O. Box 180, Summertown, TN 38483 or call (800) 695-2241 offers soyfoods, nutritional yeast, nut butters, sprouting seeds, jerkies, plus much more. Order online at <www.healthy-eating. com>; **Maine Coast Sea Vegetables**, 3 Georges Pond Road, Franklin, ME 04634. Visit <www. seaveg.com> or call (207) 565-2907; **Maine Seaweed Company**, Box 57, Steuben, ME 04680. Call (207) 546-2875 or visit <www.theseaweed man.com>; **Mendocino Sea Vegetable Company**, P.O. Box 455, Philo, CA 95466. Call (707) 895-2996 or visit <www.seaweed.net>; **Natural Lifestyle Market**, 16 Lookout Drive, Asheville, NC 28804. Visit <www. natural-lifestyle.com> or call (828) 254-9606; **Organic Provisions**,

P.O. Box 756, Richboro, PA 18954 offers organic and kosher products from various companies. Call (800) 490-0044 or visit <www.orgfood. com>; and **Shiloh Farms**, <www. shilohfarms.com>.

Organically Grown Garden Seed

High Mowing Organic Seeds, 76 Quarry Road, Wolcott, VT 05680 offers herb, vegetable, and flower seeds. Call 802-472-6174 or visit <www.highmowingseeds.com>; **Johnny's Selected Seeds**, 955 Benton Avenue, Winslow ME 04901. Call 877-564-6697 or visit <www.johnny seeds.com>; **Peaceful Valley Farm & Garden Supply**, P.O. Box 2209, Grass Valley, CA 95945 offers a wide variety of organic seeds. Call (888) 784-1722 or visit <www.grow organic.com>; and **Seeds of Change**, P.O. Box 4908, Rancho Dominquez, CA 90020 offers organic seeds that are all open-pollinated and not hybrids. Visit <www.seedsof change.com> or call (888) 762-7333.

Vegan Chocolate Lovers' Delights

Cocolate.com, search under vegan and find many options. Call (800) 396-8137; **IndulgeInChocolate.com** offers vegan chocolate. Call (877) 762-9321; **Sunspire**, offers vegan chocolate bars. Call (800) 434-4246 or visit <www.sunspire.com>; and **Wax Orchards**, P.O. Box 25448, Seattle, WA 98165, offers vegan frostings, hot cocoa, dip for strawberries, a variety of sweet fudge toppings, and a concentrated fruit juice sweetener. Visit <www.waxorchards.com> or call (800) 634-6132.

VEGAN FOOD PRODUCTS

You may have trouble finding certain vegan foods in your neighborhood. For this reason, we offer the following list of vegan products you may want to buy. Try to get your local supermarket or natural foods store to carry these products. If this fails, write to the companies and ask them how you can obtain these items. Some will mail-order or sell online.

Alternative Baking Company Inc., 3914 Kristi Court, Sacramento, CA 95827 manufactures delicious vegan cookies. Call (888) 488-9725 or visit <www.alternativebaking.com>; **Amy's Kitchen**, P.O. Box 449, Petaluma, CA 94953 produces veggie burgers, vegan pizza, black bean vegetable enchiladas, non-dairy burritos, Mexican tamale pie, roasted vegetable pocket sandwiches, toaster pops, Indian cuisine, and much more. Call (707) 568-4500 or visit <www.amys.com>; **Crofters Food Ltd.**, 7 Great North Road, Parry Sound, Ontario, Canada P2A 2X8 offers organic fruit spreads. Visit <www.croftersorganic.com> or call

(705) 746-6301; **Daiya Foods, Inc.**, makes vegan cheese that melts well. Visit <www.daiyafoods.com>; **East Wind Nut Butters**, HCR 3, Box 3370, Tecumseh, MO 65760 sells natural peanut butter, tahini, cashew butter, and almond butter, as well as organic peanut butter, organic tahini, and organic roasted peanuts. Call (417) 679-4682; **Eatem Foods Company**, Vineland Industrial Park, 1829 Gallagher Drive, Vineland, NJ 08360 offers vegan vegetable broth bases in tubs. Call (800) 683-2836 or visit <www.eatemfoods.com>; **Eden Foods**, 701 Tecumseh Road, Clinton, MI 49236 manufactures organic beans, sea vegetables, miso, various pastas, etc. Call (888) 424-3336 or visit <www.edenfoods.com>; **Edward and Sons Trading Company Inc.**, P.O. Box 1326, Carpinteria, CA 90314 offers a wide range of organic/vegan foods including canned tropical fruit, coconut products, vegan Worcestershire sauce, sprinkles for baked goods, candies, and tapioca. Call (805) 684-8500 or visit <www.edwardandsons.com>; **Ener-G Foods, Inc.**, 5960 1st Avenue South, Seattle, WA 98108 offers a vegan egg replacer and other vegan products for special diets. Visit <www.ener-g.com> or call (800) 331-5222; **Fantastic Foods, Inc.**, sells numerous products including instant refried beans, tabouli, falafel, tempura batter, nature burgers, chili, pilafs, and pasta salads. Visit <www.fantasticfoods. com>; **Field Roast Grain Meat Company**, 1440 South Jackson Street, Seattle, WA 98144 produces a wide range of alternative meats made out of gluten including loaves, deli slices, and sausage. Visit <www.fieldroast.com> or call (800) 311-9497; **Fillo Factory, Inc.**, 70 Cortland Avenue, Dumont, NJ 07628 offers spelt fillo dough, vegan assortment of appetizers, organic maple walnut baklava, etc. Call (800) OK-FILLO or visit <www.fillofactory.com>; **Jyoti Indian Cuisine**, 300 Elmwood Avenue, Sharon Hill, PA 19079 produces excellent Indian canned products. Call (610) 522-2650 or visit <www.jyotifoods.com>; **Once Again Nut Butter, Inc.**, 12 South State Street, P.O. Box 429, Nunda, NY 14517 offers organic peanut butter and tahini, as well as almond, cashew, and sunflower seed butter. Call (888) 800-8075 or visit <www.onceagainnutbutter.com>; **Parma**, P.O. Box 5563, Central Point, OR 97502 makes vegan Parmesan out of walnuts and nutritional yeast. Call (541) 665-0348 or visit <www.eatparma. com>; **Sophie's Kitchen**, 1590 Cunningham Road, Sebastopol, CA 95472 produces vegan "seafood" products. Call (877) 464-0732 or visit <www.sophieskitchen.net>; **Suzanne's Specialties, Inc.**, 40 Fulton Street, Unit 7, New Brunswick, NJ 08901 produces organic sweeteners including rice syrup and agave, as well as Ricemellow Crème. Call (800) 762-2135 or visit <www.suzannes-specialties.com>; and **Van's Natural Foods**, 3285 East Vernon Avenue, Vernon, CA 90058 produces vegan Soy/Flax Toaster Waffles and French Toast. Call (323) 585-5581 or visit <www.vansfoods.com>.

Vegan Soyfoods

Beware: Some soy cheeses contain casein, a milk product.

Chicago Vegan Foods, manufactures vegan cheese and marshmallows. Visit <www.chicagosoydairy.com> or call (630) 629-9667. Vegan Gourmet, a vegan cheese, is available from **Earth Island/Follow Your Heart Company**, P.O. Box 9400, Canoga Park, CA 91309. This company also produces vegan cream cheese, sour cream, and Vegenaise, a mayonnaise. Call (818) 725-2820 or visit <www.followyourheart.com>; Vegan cheese in American and Mozzarella flavors, cream cheese, and grated Parmesan are manufactured by **Galaxy Nutritional Foods**, 66 Whitecap Drive, North Kingstown, RI 02852. Visit <www.galaxyfoods. com>; **Earth Balance, GFA Brands**, 7102 LaVista Place, Suite 200, Niwot, CO 80503 makes a vegan non-hydrogenated, buttery spread with no *trans* fatty acids. They also offer vegan shortening and soy milk. Call (201) 421-3970 or visit <www.earthbalancenatural.com>; **Melissa's**, P.O. Box 514599, Los Angeles, CA 90051 offers a huge range of products including Soyrizo and Soy Taco, which are Mexican-style meat alternatives. Visit <www.melissas.com> or call (800) 588-0151; **Health is Wealth, Inc.**, 1051 Sykes Lane, P.O. Box 440, Williamstown, NJ 08094 manufactures Chicken Free Nuggets and Patties, as well as Buffalo Wings. Call (856) 728-1998 or visit <www.healthiswealthfoods. com>; **Boca Foods**, P.O. Box 8995, Madison, WI 53708 makes vegan burgers. Call (877) 966-8769 or visit <www.bocaburger.com>; Fat-free Smart Dogs and Tofu Pups are produced by **Lightlife Foods, Inc.**, 153 Industrial Blvd., Turner Falls, MA 01376. They also produce vegan luncheon meats and tempeh. Visit <www.lightlife.com>; Vegan Canadian Bacon, Pepperoni, and more are produced by **Yves Veggie Cuisine**, 1638 Derwent Way, Delta, British Columbia, Canada V3M 6R9. Visit <www.yvesveggie.com>; **Turtle Island Foods Inc.**, P.O. Box 176, Hood River, OR 97031 manufactures several varieties of tempeh and burgers, as well as pizza. They also produce Tofurky and Tofurky Deli Slices made from tofu and gluten, as well as Brats. Call (800) 508-8100 or visit <www.tofurky.com>; **Sol Cuisine**, 3249 Lenworth Drive, Mississauga, ON, Canada L4Z 2G6 produces organic ribs and Sol Ground. Visit <www.solcuisine.com>; **Nasoya Foods**, 1 New England Way, Ayer, MA 01432, offers Nayonaise. Call (800) Vitasoy or visit <www.nasoya.com>; Soy milk and ice cream are found in most supermarkets today. Look for EdenSoy and Edensoy Extra from **Eden Foods, Inc.**, 701 Tecumseh Road, Clinton, MI 49236; Westbrae soy milks and Soy Dream from Imagine Foods, Inc., are available from **The Hain Celestial Group**, 4600 Sleepytime Drive, Boulder, CO 80301; **Pacific Foods**, 194880 SW 97th Avenue, Tualatin, OR 97062; **Vitasoy USA Inc.**, 400 Oyster Point Blvd., Suite 201, South San Francisco, CA 94080; **Tofutti Brands, Inc.**,

50 Jackson Drive, Cranford, NJ 07016 sells Kosher vegan cream cheese and soy ice cream. Call (908) 272-2400; **Turtle Mountain**, P.O. Box 21938, Eugene, OR 97402 offers Soy Delicious frozen dessert and yogurt. Visit <www.turtlemountain.com> or call (866) 388-7853; **White Wave Foods Company**,12002 Airport Way, Broomfield, CO 80021 sells Silk soy milk, creamer, and soy yogurt. Visit <www.silksoymilk.com>; **Nancy's**, 29440 Airport Road, Eugene, OR 97402, offers vegan fruit-flavored cultured soy yogurts. Visit <www.nancysyogurt.com> or call (541) 689-2911; **Pulmuone Wild Wood Organics**, 2315 Moore Avenue, Fullerton, CA 92833 makes soy yogurt and tofu. Call (800) 588-7782 or visit <wildwoodfoods.com>; **WholeSoy and Company**, 353 Sacramento Street, Suite 1120, San Francisco, CA 94111 offers soy yogurt and cream cheese style spreads. Visit <www.wholesoyco.com>.

VEGAN VITAMINS

Freeda Vitamins, 47-25 34th Street, 3rd Floor, Long Island City, NY 11101. Visit <www.freedavitamins.com> or Call (800) 777-3737. **Vegetarian Vitamins**, 675 Forest Lakes Drive, Sterrett, AL 35147. Call (866) 211-0815 or visit <www.vegetarianvitamins.com>. (We do not suggest taking vitamins unless recommended by a doctor or nutritionist.)

CRUELTY-FREE COSMETICS
VEGAN/NOT TESTED ON ANIMALS

Note: Some mail-order and online companies sell only strictly vegan cosmetics; that is, the product has not been tested on animals and contains no animal products. However, many companies sell cosmetics that have not been tested on animals, but may contain animal products. The following companies often indicate which items are vegan.

Aubrey Organics, 4419 N. Manhattan Avenue, Tampa, FL 33614. Call (800) 282-7394 or visit <www.aubrey-organics.com>; **Ecco Bella**, 623 Eagle Rock Avenue, Suite 381, West Orange, NJ 07052. Visit <www.eccobella.com>; **Kiss My Face Corporation**, P.O. Box 224, Gardiner, NY 12525 or call (800) 262-KISS; **Logona USA, Inc.**, Call (800) 225-6111 or visit <www.logona-usa.com>; **LUSH**, Call (888) 733-5874 or visit <www.lushusa.com>; **Rainbow Research**, 170 Wilbur Place, Bohemia, NY 11716. Call (800) 722-9595 or visit <www.rainbow research.com>; **Simmons Natural Bodycare**, 42295 Highway 36, Bridgeville, CA 95526. Call (707) 777-1920; **Sombra Cosmetics Inc.**, 5951 Office Blvd. NE, Albuquerque, NM 87109. Call (800) 225-3963 or visit <www.sombrausa.com>; and **Vegan Essentials**, 1701 Pearl Street,

Unit 8, Waukesha, WI 53186. Visit <www.veganessentials. com> or call (866) 88-VEGAN.

In addition, the following groups offer a list of cruelty-free cosmetics: **American Anti-Vivisection Society (AAVS)**, 801 Old York Road, Suite 204, Jenkintown, PA 19046. Visit <www.aavs.org>; **The Humane Society of the United States (HSUS)**, 2100 L Street NW, Washington, D.C. 20037; and **People for the Ethical Treatment of Animals (PETA)**, 501 Front Street, Norfolk, VA 23501. Visit <www.peta.org>.

ENVIRONMENTALLY SOUND VEGAN HOUSEHOLD PRODUCTS

Allens Naturally, visit <www.allensnaturally.com> or call (800) 352-8971; **Bi-O-Kleen**, visit <www.biokleenhome.com> or call (800) 477-0188; **Citra-Solv**, P.O. Box 2597, Danbury, CT 06813. Call (800) 343-6588 or visit <www.citrasolv.com>; **Dr. Bronner's**, P.O. Box 28, Escondido, CA 92033. Call (877) 786-3649 or visit <www.drbronner. com>; **Earth Friendly Products**, 44 Green Bay Road, Winnetka, IL 60093. Call (800) 336-3749 or visit <www.ecos.com>; **Ecover**, visit <www.ecover.com> or call (800) 449-4925; **Planet Inc.**, call (800) 858-8449 or visit <www.planetinc.com>; **Seventh Generation Inc.**, 60 Lake Street, Burlington, VT 05401. Call (800) 456-1191 or visit <www.seventh generation.com>; **Sun and Earth Inc.**, 221 King Manor Drive, King of Prussia, PA 19406. Call (866) 389-7967 or visit <www.sunandearth. com>; and **Tomahawk Live Trap Company**, P.O. Box 155, Hazelhurst, WI 54531. Call (800) 272-8727 or visit <www.livetrap.com>.

ECO-FRIENDLY CLOTHING CONTAINING NO ANIMAL PRODUCTS

Clothes Made From Scrap, P. O. Box 149084, Orlando, FL 32814 markets a line of apparel and accessories made from recycled material including plastic soda bottles and reclaimed cotton. Call (386) 405-4680 or visit <www.clothesmadefromscrap.com>; **Donna Salyers' Fabulous Furs**, 25 West Robbins Street, Covington, KY 41011 offers a wide variety of fake fur coats and other items. They can be reached at (800) 848-4650 or visit <www.fabulousfurs.com>; **Earth Creations**, 3056 Mountainview Way, Bessemer, AL 35020 produces clothing that is clay-dyed and made from hemp and organic cotton. Call (800) 792-9868 or visit <www.earthcreations.net>; **The Ethical Man**, sells men's coats,

wallets, belts, ties, bow ties, etc. online at <www.theethicalman.com>;
KidBean.com, 2400 NE 10th Avenue, Pompano Beach, FL 33064
offers organic cotton and hemp clothing for kids, Visit <www.kidbean.
com>; **Lands' End, Inc.**, 1 Lands' End Lane, Dodgeville, WI 53595 and
LL Bean, Inc., 15 Casco St., Freeport, ME 04033 sell cotton items;
however, not all items are vegan; **Maggie's Functional Organics**, 306
West Cross Street, Ypsilanti, MI 48197 sells organic cotton knitwear
including socks, camisoles, t-shirts, tights, and more. For details call
(800) 609-8593 or visit <www.maggiesorganics.com>; **Pangea**, 2381
Lewis Ave., Rockville, MD 20851 offers a wide range of vegan items
including shoes, belts, bags, personal care items, and much more. Call
(800) 340-1200 or visit <www.veganstore.com>; **Tomorrow's World**,
201 West Ocean View Avenue, Norfolk, Virginia 23503 offers a wide
range of cotton and hemp clothing, bedding, bath items, and more. They
can be reached at (800) 229-7571 or visit <www.tomorrowsworld.com>;
Vegetarian Shoes offers non-leather footwear, as well as non-leather
jackets. Visit <www.vegetarian-shoes.co.uk>; and **The Vegetarian Site**,
P.O. Box 222, Glastonbury, CT 06033 offers clothing, footwear, and
much more. Call (860) 519-1918 or visit <www.the vegetariansite.com>.

PERSONAL CARE PRODUCTS

Note: Some of the following companies do mail-order while others offer
their items in natural foods stores and other retail outlets.

Clear Conscience, P.O. Box 17855, Arlington, VA 22216 offers cruelty-
free contact lens solution. Visit <www.clearconscience.com> or call
(800) 595-9592; **Clearly Natural**, P.O. Box 750024, Petaluma, CA
94975 manufactures vegan glycerine-based soaps. Call (800) 451-7096
or visit <www.clearlynaturalsoaps.com>; **Harvest Soaps**, P.O. Box 7175,
Watchung, NJ 07069 offers soap for adults and infants. Visit <www.
harvestsoaps.com> or call (908) 320-7076; **Nature's Gate**, 9200 Mason
Avenue, Chatsworth, CA 91311 sells herbal shampoos and condition-
ers, toothpastes, and more. Call (800) 421-1223 or visit <natures-
gate.com>; **Rainbow Research Corporation**, 170 Wilbur Place,
Bohemia, NY 11716 carries the Baby Oh Baby line, which includes diaper treatment cream, shampoo, soaps, and more. Call (800) 722-9595
or visit <www.rainbowresearch.com>; and **Tom's of Maine**, Inc., 302
Lafayette Center, Kennebunk, ME 04043 sells toothpaste, deodorant,
soap, shampoo, mouthwash, and shaving cream. Call (800) 367-8667
or visit <www.tomsofmaine.com>.

EDUCATIONAL MATERIALS

Bullfrog Films, Inc., P.O. Box 149, Oley, PA 19547 is the distributor of vegetarian, animal rights, and sustainable development films/DVDs. Call (800) 543-3764 for information; **Center for Teaching Peace**, 4501 Van Ness Street NW, Washington, DC 20016 offers lectures on non-violence, vegetarianism, animal rights, environmental concerns, etc.; **Co-op America's National Green Pages**, 1612 K Street NW, #600, Washington, DC 20006 or call (800) 58-GREEN. You'll find a terrific list of environmental/vegetarian friendly businesses; and **The Vegetarian Site** sells several vegetarian and animal rights DVDs. Visit <www.vegetariansite.com>.

RECOMMENDED READING LIST
VEGAN COOKBOOKS AND NUTRITION BOOKS

Becoming Vegan. By Brenda Davis, R.D. and Vesanto Melina, M.S., R.D. Book Publishing Company, 2000.

Conveniently Vegan. By Debra Wasserman. The Vegetarian Resource Group, 1997.

Diet, Life Expectancy, and Chronic Disease: Studies of Seventh-day Adventists and Other Vegetarians. By Gary E. Fraser. Oxford University Press, 2003.

The Dietitian's Guide to Vegetarian Diets. By Reed Mangels, Virginia Messina, and Mark Messina. Jones & Bartlett Learning, 2011.

The Everything Vegan Pregnancy Book. By Reed Mangels. Adams Media, 2011.

The Joy of Vegan Baking. By Colleen Patrick-Goudreau. Fair Winds Press. 2007.

The Lowfat Jewish Vegetarian Cookbook. By Debra Wasserman. The Vegetarian Resource Group, 1994.

Meatless Meals for Working People. By Debra Wasserman and Charles Stahler. The Vegetarian Resource Group, 2004.

More Fabulous Beans. By Barb Bloomfield. Book Publishing Company, 2004.

The New Farm Vegetarian Cookbook. Edited by Louise Hagler and Dorothy R. Bates. Book Publishing Company, 1989.

No Cholesterol Passover Recipes. By Debra Wasserman and Charles Stahler. The Vegetarian Resource Group, 1994.

Plant Based Nutrition and Health. By Stephen Walsh. The Vegan Society, 2003.

Raising Vegetarian Children. By Joanne Stepaniak and Vesanto Melina, M.S., R.D. The McGraw-Hill Companies, 2003.

The Ultimate Uncheese Cookbook. By Joanne Stepaniak. Book Publishing Company, 2003.

Vegan Brunch. By Isa Chandra Moskowitz. DeCapo Press, 2009.

Vegan Comfort Food. By Alicia C. Simpson. The Experiment, 2009.

Vegan for Life. By Jack Norris, R.D. and Virginia Messina, M.P.H., R.D. DaCapo Press, 2011.

Vegan Handbook. Edited by Debra Wasserman and Reed Mangels. The Vegetarian Resource Group, updated 2005.

The Vegan Kitchen. By Freya Dinshah. American Vegan Society, 1992.

Vegan Meals for One or Two. By Nancy Berkoff, Ed.D., R.D. The Vegetarian Resource Group, 2001.

Vegan Menu for People with Diabetes. By Nancy Berkoff, Ed.D., R.D. The Vegetarian Resource Group, 2004.

Vegan Microwave Cookbook. By Nancy Berkoff, Ed.D., R.D. The Vegetarian Resource Group, 2003.

Vegan Seafood. By Nancy Berkoff, Ed.D., R.D. The Vegetarian Resource Group, 2008.

Vegan in Volume. By Nancy Berkoff, Ed.D., R.D. The Vegetarian Resource Group, 2000.

Vegans Know How to Party. Nancy Berkoff, Ed.D., R.D. The Vegetarian Resource Group, 2011.

MISCELLANEOUS BOOKS

The Inner World of Farm Animals. By Amy Hatkoff. Harry N. Abrams, 2009.

Mad Cowboy - Plain Truth from the Cattle Rancher Who Won't Eat Meat. By Howard Lyman with Glen Merzer. Scribner, 2001.

Slaughterhouse. By Gail A. Eisnitz. Prometheus Books, 1997.

Vegetarian America: A History. By Karen and Michael Iacobbo. Praeger Publishers, 2004.

Visit The Vegetarian Resource Group's website at <www.vrg.org>. Here you'll find a wide range of vegan recipes, as well as articles on many different subjects related to a vegan lifestyle.

INDEX

INDEX OF TABLES

JOIN THE VEGETARIAN RESOURCE GROUP
RECEIVE VEGETARIAN JOURNAL

The Vegetarian Resource Group (VRG) is a non-profit organization educating the public about the various aspects of vegetarianism, which is the abstinence of meat, fish, and fowl, as well as veganism, which is the abstinence of all animal products including eggs and dairy products. The group publishes *Vegetarian Journal*, a 36-page publication, which includes vegan recipes, product reviews, nutrition hotline, scientific updates, and much more. VRG also publishes other books and brochures, and sponsors events open to the public.

* MEMBERSHIP APPLICATION *

NAME _____

ADDRESS_____

_____ ZIP _____

TELEPHONE_____

Send a $25 check or postal money order ($32 for Canada and Mexico; $42 for other foreign countries) to The Vegetarian Resource Group, P.O. Box 1463, Baltimore, MD 21203. Members receive *Vegetarian Journal*. Call (410) 366-8343 9 am to 5 pm Eastern Time with questions. You can also charge your membership with a Visa/Mastercard. Our e-mail address is vrg@vrg.org, our fax number is (410) 366-8804, and our website is <www.vrg.org>.

OTHER BOOKS PUBLISHED BY
THE VEGETARIAN RESOURCE GROUP

Conveniently Vegan: Learn how to prepare meals with all the new natural foods products found in stores today. Includes 150 vegan recipes using convenience foods along with fresh fruits and vegetables, menu ideas, product sources, and food definitions. Cost: $15

Vegan Meals for One or Two: We've designed recipes to serve one or two so that you can realistically use ingredients the way they come packaged in stores. Cost: $15

Vegan Microwave Cookbook: Many recipes in this book take under 10 minutes to prepare. Others are appropriate for entertaining. Cost: $17

Vegan in Volume: This book serves up 125 quantity recipes for every occasion. Good for dinner parties, catered events, weddings, college food service, restaurants, and more. Cost: $20

Vegan Menu for People with Diabetes: These menus make following a vegan diet easy both for people with diabetes and those who are concerned about developing diabetes. 32 vegan recipes included. Cost: $10

The Lowfat Jewish Vegetarian Cookbook: Features 150 lowfat vegan recipes from around the world. Cost: $15

Vegan Handbook: Over 200 vegan recipes including egg-free cakes, Thanksgiving ideas, vegan pancakes, feeding vegan children, etc. Also find a senior's guide, sports nutrition, vegetarian history, non-leather resources, menus, and much more. Cost: $20

Vegans Know How to Party: Includes over 465 recipes, including appetizers, soups, salads, ethnic cuisine, desserts, etc. Cost: $25

Additional copies of Simply Vegan are $15.95 per book. Inquire about quantity discounts on all our books for stores and non-profit groups.

**<u>*Please add $6 for shipping on orders under $25 in the USA.</u>
Send check to The Vegetarian Resource Group, P.O. Box, 1463, Baltimore, MD 21203 or call (410) 366-8343 9 am to 5 pm EST to charge your order. Our fax number is (410) 366-8804, our email address is vrg@vrg.org, and our website is <www.vrg.org>.**